Gina
by Willd
Mc Gowrin

March 2019
at Tip Grand

SEVEN STEPS

to BECOMING a
HEALTHY CHRISTIAN LEADER

Doug Munton

VMI Publishers

where i

Dedication

This book is dedicated to the wonderful people of First Baptist Church of O'Fallon, Illinois. You are a delight to share the journey of faith with. May God continue to work in our hearts together.

Acknowledgements

I want to express my grateful appreciation to the following people. . .

To my wife, Vickie, who is my dearest friend and greatest supporter. She is my confidant, encourager and ministry partner.

To my children, Josiah, Emily, Rachel and Jarrett, who make my life so much fun. I am thankful God let me be their dad.

To my parents, who first taught me the joys and responsibilities of faith.

To Bill Carmichael and VMI publishers, who believed in the value of this book. Your encouragement means so much.

To Larry Richmond and the wonderful staff at First Baptist Church, O'Fallon, IL, who live out healthy Christian leadership every day.

To Steve Hawkins, Malcolm McDow, Alvin Reid and Randy Singer, who gave their valuable time to read the manuscript, and offer suggestions.

CONTENTS

PREFACE

My first real ministry responsibility was a little overwhelming! I was home from college for the summer and was asked to lead the children's worship service and bus ministry at my home church. Over the next three months I experienced laughter, tears and a lice epidemic. It was exciting, frustrating and frightening all at the same time. I loved God, I knew the basics of our programs, but I did not have a clue about leadership.

I have written this book to help you become the best Christian leader possible. Perhaps, like me, you have experienced the highs and lows that come with ministry responsibilities. You teach a Sunday School class or have become a deacon. You are a pastor, staff member or missionary. You love God. You know the program. But you want to become the healthy Christian leader God wants you to be.

Healthy Christian leadership is the great need of the hour. Our churches and ministries need more than new programs and methodologies. We need men and women who are healthy, vibrant, godly leaders. We need well-balanced leaders who model for us effective spiritual leadership.

Join me in exploring seven characteristics every Christian leader needs in his or her ministry arsenal. These steps can help you discover the joy, excitement and effectiveness ministry leadership is intended to produce.

Doug Munton

CHAPTER ONE

DEEPEN YOUR INTIMACY WITH GOD

*Healthy Christian leaders develop and maintain a close,
vibrant relationship with God.*

Carl and Louise were my landlords, neighbors, fellow church members and friends. I was a young pastor, and they were like surrogate grandparents to my wife and me. We loved both of them dearly. But they did have one unusual characteristic- especially considering they had been married for more than fifty years. They fought like cats and dogs!

Rarely did I hear them speak to each other that it wasn't with hostility and bitterness. Though they never spoke a harsh word to my family or me in the years we lived next door, they couldn't seem to be civil to each other. Perhaps just as surprising was the way they ignored the basic principles of marriage.

They lived in the same house but rarely ate meals together. They slept in different bedrooms. They came to church in different vehicles. They lived separate lives.

One event seemed to characterize their relationship. One summer Carl went through a period of extended illness. He was in the hospital for a time and came home to continue his recuperation. As his pastor, I checked on him occasionally. One day I saw Louise outside and stopped to inquire how Carl was recovering. Louise replied, "Well, I talked to him last week, and he seemed to be doing better." I thought in amazement, *Last week? You talked to him last week? You live in the same house and weekly communication seems to be often enough?*

Over time I discovered a little about their early life. Carl worked on her father's farm as a hired hand. Louise thought he was a handsome young man. Carl couldn't help but notice the farmer's pretty young daughter. The two began to "court."

Carl came over to the house in the evenings and played checkers with Louise's father. Apparently, Carl lost many games due to lack of concentration. He kept sneaking peaks at Louise. He thought she was so beautiful. When the night got late, Dad suggested Carl should be leaving. Louise always walked him to the door just to be near him, then lingered on the porch as he slowly walked away, casting wistful glances back her way.

They sat near each other at church. There were always other people around, but at least they could exchange a few words and looks. They loved those church socials when they could find a few moments to talk alone together.

The courting became more serious. Intentions were made known. Carl asked Louise to be his bride and she joyfully accepted! They were married in front of family and friends in that country church and Carl thought she was the most beautiful bride in all the world. Louise blushed with happiness at being Carl's wife. They were in love!

But somewhere down the line that love faded. They stopped courting. They stopped communicating. They stopped eating and sleeping together. "I talked to him last week, and he seemed to be doing better." Oh, they were still married. Their legal status of husband and wife remained unchanged. But their love had grown cold.

Something very much like that happened to the church in Ephesus. Jesus said to them, "You have forsaken your first love." (Rev. 2:4) They seemed to be a church that had it all. They were active, moral, religious. Yet Jesus said they had a problem: they had lost the intimacy they once enjoyed with him.

Christian leaders can make the same mistake made by Carl and Louise or believers at Ephesus. They can go through the motions and activities of religion without the intimacy God desires. They are still church members, still leaders in ministry, but they have forsaken their first love.

Healthy leadership begins with closeness to God. Some people begin ministry with ulterior motives. They are in it for self-advancement or as a means of gaining wealth. They are "wolves in sheep clothing". I think, however, that most people who become ministry leaders do so because they love God and want to serve him effectively. They begin to serve others, share their faith or provide leadership to some ministry as an outgrowth of their intimate relationship with Christ. But sometimes those who began their service with great spiritual fervor continue their service long after the passion is gone.

Can you lead in ministry without intimacy with God? Sadly, the answer seems to be a surprising "yes." Unfortunately, examples abound. But you cannot be the leader God wants you to be without closeness with him. You may be successful numerically or be praised by others. But eventually the lack of spiritual strength that comes from a lack of spiritual intimacy will be your downfall.

I suggest to you that your "success" will only be short-term without a commitment to intimacy with God. Your ministry leadership will be like the house built upon the sand. And eventually, maybe not immediately, but eventually, it is going to rain. Hard!

Can a person of your caliber lose intimacy with God? Absolutely! Don't make the mistake of thinking, "That couldn't happen to me." The subtle, almost imperceptible drift from God will happen to anyone who lives an unguarded life. It can happen to the talented, the gifted and the successful. Anyone. You are not immune. Especially if you think you are.

I can unwittingly begin that drift from God. I can get too busy to read my Bible or pray. Ministry concerns can sometimes keep me from spending time with God. I can allow the work of ministry to keep me from the work of God in me.

Many Christian leaders don't really want to talk about spiritual depth. They prefer to focus on programs and methodology and activity. And those issues are important, but God is not merely concerned with what you do. He is concerned with who you are. Build a solid foundation upon your relationship with God and your potential for significant ministry leadership is limitless. But take a shortcut around spiritual development and you will face the inevitable roadblock of God's discipline.

Spirituality is not the only factor in healthy Christian leadership. I have known godly people who were ineffective leaders. They were poor Sunday School teachers or weak leaders in ministry or ineffective as pastors and missionaries. Personal devotion to God is not a guarantee for being a strong spiritual leader. But there is no substitute for it. In the long run, no amount of ability or innovation can cover for a lack of godliness.

One of the great things about intimacy with God is that it is not restricted by our frail abilities. Limited intellectual skills need not be a hindrance to closeness with God. Lack of training or education does not keep us from his presence. Meager talents will not hinder our relationship with the Almighty.

It is just as wonderful to realize that great intellect, the best in educational training and bushels of talents need not hinder us from intimacy with God, either. God is not overly impressed with our abilities and talents since they are gifts he gives us anyway. Our resume does not overwhelm him. If you have been blessed with great intellect, praise God. If you have had excellent educational opportunities, thank the Lord. If you have been gifted beyond measure, thank God for his grace. But never allow those things to substitute for the closeness God wants with you every day of your life. Healthy church leaders know better.

Intimacy and Holiness

If you ask the average person in an American church today to complete the sentence "God is _____," how do you think they would fill in the blank? I think most American Christians today would say, "God is love." There would be other answers, but probably most would emphasize God's love. But if you had asked the same question in American churches two hundred years ago, I think you would have gotten a different answer. Most American Christians of that era would probably have answered the question by saying, "God is holy."

Both answers are right. God is love and God is holy. But

different generations have emphasized different things. We might look back at the writings and sermons of previous generations and say they did not sufficiently emphasize God's love. I wonder if previous generations of church leaders might look askance at our writings and our sermons and our teaching. Might they not say to us, if they were able, "You emphasized God's love and for that you are to be commended. But where was the reminder of God's holiness?"

Holiness and closeness to God work together. God expects his people to be holy. 1 Peter 1: 15-16 (NIV) states, *"But just as he who called you is holy, so be holy in all you do; for it is written: 'Be holy, because I am holy."* It is the nature of God to be holy. God expects his followers to reflect that nature. When we disobey God, when we live unholy lives, we are separated from the intimacy God desires.

My wife and I have four children. (Or is it five? No, I just checked again, it's only four!) When they disobey us, (though it is hard to imagine in a pastor's family!) it causes some problems. We remain in relationship. I am still their father. They are still my sons or daughters. But something happens to the fellowship. The disobedience causes a problem in our fellowship together. Some form of discipline (a highly unpopular subject with my children) will likely follow.

In a similar fashion, our holiness, or lack thereof, affects our fellowship with God. While God continues to love us despite our disobedience, our closeness to God is disrupted. The relationship remains, but the fellowship is affected. Some form of God's discipline (a highly unpopular subject with God's children) will follow.

The Importance of Consistency. We've all seen the kind of roller coaster rides many people take spiritually. They go to a seminar, or a camp, or some other event that touches their heart. They make promises to God. "I'll never sin again!" "I will change my ways!" "I'll stop cussin' and chewin' and drinkin' and I'll get grandma to quit, too!" And they mean it. They mend their ways—at least for a while.

But before long they are back into the same old mess they were in before. Why? Sometimes the promises only last as long as the feelings. When the emotions wear out the resolve wears out. Maybe we need a special cheer in Christian circles. You know, have some folks call out letters for the crowd to repeat. Perhaps throw a cheerleader or two in the air. Spell out C-O-N-S-I-S-T-E-N-C-Y for all to hear.

Consistency isn't very glamorous. We are much more impressed by the decision, the moment of commitment. But consistency is essential for the kind of intimacy with God that we desire. Consistency is hard work. It takes effort to be consistent in a life devoted to the Lord over the long haul. Yet consistency carries benefits that can be gained in no other way.

Integrity doesn't work without consistency. One of the best definitions of integrity is "who you are when no one is looking."[1] You can't pick and choose when you want to be a person of integrity. You don't have integrity only when someone is watching. If you have integrity, you are, by definition, consistent.

I learned a good lesson in consistency in college. Or maybe I should say that I watched a good lesson in consistency in college. My roommate at Wheaton College was Brian Edwards. Brian and I are different in many ways. He grew up on the East Coast. I'm from the Midwest. I played football at Wheaton. He wasn't in any sports. He was a math major. I get nauseous at the thought of algebra. Brian was more contemplative and serious. I am more obnoxious. He is an actuary. I am a reactuary. (That word doesn't seem to want to make it through spell check!)

Every day I watched as Brian had his "quiet time." He spent time each morning reading the Bible and praying. My devotional life had always been hit and miss. I read the Bible when I remembered to, or felt like it, or when the "pangs of conscience" irritated me enough. Brian read the Bible every day. Period.

After a while I began to wonder if maybe Brian was on to something. Maybe consistency was paying off. He seemed to be growing spiritually more rapidly than I was. Perhaps I should give consistency a try. So I did.

Now admittedly, I struggled with consistency. (I still do!) But that step toward an every day, feel-like-it-or-not time alone with God was a critical turning point in my spiritual development. It made a real difference. Bring on that consistency cheer!

Beware of Scandalous Sin. We have seen more than enough scandalous activities among church leaders in recent years. We have watched as some high profile ministry leaders have been caught in immorality. For the most part, these events have seemed far removed from my world. I could ignore them or watch with detached disdain.

But this one was different. It was during my seminary days. The pastor in this scandal was older than I, but he was still relatively young. He was dynamic and handsome. I admired his skill, his grace, his manner. His messages were inspirational and moving. He knew what he was doing and where he was going. He had an air of sophistication about him. I remember thinking: "There's a guy who would make a good model for a young minister. Maybe some day I could be a sophisticated pastor like him."

When it was made public that he had been involved in multiple cases of adultery, I was deeply hurt. How could anyone with such ability, such charisma, fall in such a way? That is when I realized scandalous sin could happen to anyone who lives an unguarded life. I suppose I knew that before, but now I *knew* that!

That man had been, I imagine, an idealistic young seminary student. He had dreamed of doing great things for God. He had prayed that God would make him holy. But at some point he turned a corner. At some point his life went unguarded. And then, at some point, he broke his wedding vows, he broke his spiritual vows, and he committed adultery. And he brought derision to the name of his Savior.

How long, I wondered, had he lived in hypocrisy, worried his secret might be revealed and his career and reputation endangered? How long had he lived with the lie and the guilt and the shame? A fellow pastor reportedly asked him some direct questions: "How did you preach the next Sunday after committing adultery? How were you able to stand before those people who trusted you and preach God's word?" He answered, "You do what you've gotta do."

So that's it? You commit adultery or embezzle money or lie through your teeth and nothing changes? You just do what you've gotta do? You prepare to teach that Sunday School class because that's what you do. You lead that women's ministry meeting because that's what you do. You lead that Bible study because that's what you do. But inside the hypocrisy is killing you.

"Wait a minute," you say. "Sin is sin. You can't categorize some sins as worse than others." There is truth to that. All sin is terrible. All sin separates us from God. All sin, even the so-called "small" sin, condemns us before God. Why speak of scandalous sin? For two reasons. Some sins are of such a nature that even those outside the body of Christ can recognize the seriousness of the offense. Paul said to the Corinthian church, "It is actually reported that there is sexual immorality among you, and of a kind that does not occur even among pagans." (I Cor.5:1) Even those who are not believers are able to recognize the hypocrisy and shame of these actions. The church and the name of Christ were maligned as a result. These sins may be called *scandalous sins*.

Secondly, scandalous sins almost always entail multiple sins. Before the adultery takes place, one must normally allow lust to have a free reign in one's life. Before embezzlement occurs, greed or envy must first go unchecked. Usually, scandalous sins are the culmination of a series of unrepentant "small" sins.

A wise person recognizes the danger and damage of sin. Scandalous sin not only damages personally but corporately. The name of Christ is dishonored, even scorned. Witness and ministry are more difficult. The wounds that are caused are deeper and often slower to heal. God wants followers to learn to deal with sin in a more positive manner.

Dealing with Temptation. Temptation and sin are not

synonyms. You can be tempted and choose not to sin. Jesus himself was tempted yet was without sin. (See Hebrews 4:15) Temptation is merely the moment of decision between obedience and disobedience. But while temptation is not sin, it is certainly dangerous and should not be taken lightly.

The old story of the wealthy woman hiring a chauffeur illustrates it well. She interviewed three candidates for the job. She asked each how close he could get to the edge of a cliff without going over. The first candidate estimated he could get to within one foot. The second candidate estimated he could get to within six inches. But the third candidate got the job when he responded by saying he tried to stay as far from the edge of cliffs as possible!

Anyone who flirts with temptation is playing with fire. There is a reason why the Bible tells us to flee sin. (See I Cor. 6:18, 10:14, I Tim. 6:11, II Tim. 2:22) Sin is as dangerous as a great chasm. The edge of the cliff is a dangerous place to hang around.

One of the most valuable tools for dealing with temptation and sin is an accountability group. A group of peers who can ask questions and who are not impressed by your trite responses can be invaluable to your victory over sin. If it had done nothing else, Promise Keepers would be worth great effort and cost just because of its emphasis on small groups of men holding each other accountable.

Men have been nervous historically about small groups. Too "touchy-feely for our blood" they have argued. But when you are more concerned about being good fathers and husbands than about appearances of machismo, you recognize the benefits of being held accountable by others.

I was a young pastor and seminary student attending a big Christian conference with my wife. It was held in Las Vegas. I had never seen anything like Las Vegas. I'm from small towns. There were *casinos* in Las Vegas bigger than some of my boyhood towns. There were *neon signs* bigger than some of those towns. And everywhere there was gambling. Little old ladies poured quarter after quarter into the ravenous mouths of slot machines.

Four other seminary students and their wives were there with my wife, Vickie, and me. The conference was an inspiration to us as well as a temporary escape from responsibilities as doctoral students and pastors. We all went out to eat together one evening. We were having a great time. The cheap food was definitely my favorite part of Las Vegas! We were laughing, enjoying the meal and company.

Someone happened to notice a relatively famous conference participant sitting at the table next to us. A Christian celebrity! My wife and I had heard him speak. We had been inspired by his words. I suppose we considered him something of a spiritual hero.

That's what made the next few moments so uncomfortable. We noticed this Christian leader acting in a way we felt was inappropriate. It wasn't murder or anything, but he was acting in ways we felt he shouldn't. Our group commented on the activities taking place, unsure of how to react. Then my wife went into action.

You have to understand my wife's personality. She is not by nature confrontational. But she felt so strongly about what was happening at the next table that she went directly to the minister and spoke with him. More distressing than his original activities was the way he blew off Vickie's concerns. "How dare she question him!" was the impression he gave. It was a discouraging series of events, and our group left the restaurant downcast. We were hurt to see a man we admired and looked up to seem so shallow and calloused. We were not entirely surprised when we read some weeks later that he had left his wife for another woman.

That night we met together in our hotel room and began to pray. We realized that his attitude of unconcern could one day be our attitude. Our zeal for holiness could wane. Our commitment to integrity in life could falter. And it scared us.

We formed a group that has met together every year since then. We meet together to pray, to hold each other accountable, to be gut-level honest with each other. That group of men and their wives has been incredibly valuable to Vickie and me. We know they love us, they care for us, and they are not impressed by us. They can ask us anything. We can do the same with them. We husbands frequently talk together about issues that confront us.

I wonder if you have a group like that. Is there someone in your life you can talk to about your victories and defeats? Someone who is not afraid to ask you about lust or covetousness or unresolved anger? If not, perhaps you should begin a search for a group you can minister with and to. Find a group that will love you, support you and challenge you. It could be a front line defense against falling to temptation and sin. Accountability could be a means by which you begin to discover real victory in your spiritual life.

The battle with temptation must be fought. Every Christian leader will face temptation. Some will fight the good fight and find God's victory. Some will succumb and miss God's best. You make the decision about which it will be.

Intimacy and a Devotional Life

I was a sleepy college student. Have a quiet time with the Lord each morning? It just didn't seem possible. There were too many late-night papers and midnight discussions to get up in time to read the Bible each morning. I couldn't spend time in prayer in the mornings, I reasoned, not with intense midnight foosball games.

I mentioned earlier the example of my college roommate. Through Brian's example and my own spiritual longing, I began to spend time each morning reading the Bible and praying. The effort began to pay off.

As I began to gain a more consistent pattern of daily devotions, my closeness to God began to improve. There were times, quite honestly, when I got little out of my Bible reading. But I also experienced moments, sometimes quite unexpectedly, when God spoke to my heart in very significant ways. Often I began my devotions out of a sense of duty only to discover at some point a great sense of joy in the spiritual journey.

I must admit I don't always feel like having a quiet time with God. After years of quiet times and years of vocational ministry, I still don't always feel like having a devotional time. But, by being obedient and consistent, I often find my feelings come along. My intimacy with God grows as I spend time in his word. A sense of closeness often follows the activity of a devotional life.

Intimacy in Prayer. Let's face it. Prayer, especially public prayer, can sometimes be intimidating. I have seen grown men, unafraid of bulls and bullies, tremble at the thought of praying out loud. When I was the new pastor of a small church in Texas, it was our custom to call on someone at the end of the service to dismiss us in prayer. One Sunday I called on one of the men, a grizzly old retired sheriff who was a regular attender, to lead us in prayer. He responded by uttering the words, "Pass, please."

For a moment I was unsure whether I was at a church service or in a card game. My mind raced to decide what to do next. Recovering, I called on someone else to pray (after all, the man had said "please"!) and then went to speak with him. This tough old lawman told me of his deathly fear of praying in front of people and asked me kindly to never call his name for public prayer again.

I wonder if that fear of prayer is limited to public prayer? Maybe there are many who spend too little time in prayer to feel any sense of intimacy in their prayer lives. They are afraid, perhaps, that their prayers will "sound funny" to God. Maybe God expects to hear more words and phrases like "thee" or "bestowed upon" and they won't get it right.

There is no cure for a lack of intimacy in prayer, like time spent in prayer. God loves to hear us when we pray. We are encouraged at numerous points by God to "Call to me . . .".[2] Among the most challenging verses in the Bible is I Thessalonians 5:17, which says, "Pray continually." God desires us to be in an attitude of prayer all the time.

In 1995 our church experienced what I believe was a

time of genuine revival.³ One of the results of that revival time was a much greater intimacy in prayer. It seemed so natural to pray. Prayer seemed to take on more significance to us, and we desired to pray more than ever before. Our passion for prayer grew, and our prayers became more passionate. Never had my prayer life been more intimate.

How cold our prayer can become! It can become a duty or obligation rather than a privilege. God desires intimacy with us, which includes a vibrant prayer life. God loves for us to speak with him about the issues, concerns and joys of our lives.

One of the ways intimacy in a marriage is maintained is through frequent communication. Have you ever seen (or been!) the husband who comes home from work, grunts at the family and spends the next several hours staring at a television screen? It's not the kind of stuff that produces legends of family intimacy. Families need healthy communication to be healthy families. What's more, many families are desperately longing for the kind of emotional intimacy that comes with talking frequently together.

God longs for spiritual intimacy with you through prayer. Make it a frequent part of your life. Pray while you drive to work, mow the lawn or jog. Spend time with the Lord during your morning quiet time and when you go to sleep.

But frequency of prayer is not enough. On occasion, as I pray with my kids at bedtime, I find myself saying something without thinking. I have thanked God for the food, even though we aren't having a meal, just bedtime! It reminds me how easy it is for my prayers to become rote and routine.

Here's a novel idea: Words ought to mean something. The words I say in prayer ought to have some meaning behind them. I am talking to God. What I say must come from my heart and my mind and not just from my lips. God is not listening for the number of your words but for the meaning of your words.⁴

Intimacy in Bible Reading. Just today, I was reading in my daily devotions from I Chronicles 11 about David and his mighty men. David longingly remarked how good it would taste to drink the water from the well in Bethlehem. You know how you get used to the taste of water from your home. Nothing else tastes quite as good. But there were enemy forces between David and his hometown. Three men overheard David say these words. They decided to do something about it. They broke through the enemy lines and scooped up a dipper full of water from Bethlehem. They brought it to David who was overwhelmed by their love. He poured the water out as a drink offering to the Lord because he was so impressed by the actions of these brave men.

I have read through the Bible many times, and I know I have read this story before. But this time, the story "hit me." What an amazing act of courage! What an amazing act of love! Instead of acting as though he deserved this kind of loyalty, David was humbled by it. Why can't I be more like those brave and faithful men? Why can't I be more humble and worshipful when honored?

God uses his Word to draw us closer to him. There is a power to his Word. It changes lives and hearts. It changes our perspectives and actions. The old time preachers understood this.

My grandmother died when she was in her nineties. She had served the Lord faithfully and fully and was ready to go home to the Lord. The pastor who preached her funeral service was not much younger than she was. For years he had preached God's Word. He had studied for messages and Sunday school lessons. He had read the Bible many times over.

During the service this older minister recited from memory a passage of Scripture. It was a familiar one for funeral services, one he had used many times, I am sure. But he did not just read it. He quoted it.

"Well," you say, "if he had used it many times before, it is not too surprising he could quote it." True. Except, that he quoted it from a newer translation of the Bible that was not even printed until he was well into his sixties!

This pastor, in his sixties or so, decided to take the time to memorize a portion of God's word in a new translation. Something about his Bible study must have stayed fresh and alive. Apparently his study of God's Word was more than just duty. There was a dynamic enthusiasm that characterized his treatment of the Bible.

Spiritual leaders who want to maintain closeness to the Lord are deeply involved in God's Word. It is still fresh and alive because they read it, study it and memorize it. Let the Bible be a part of your life. As you spend time reading God's love letter to you, you will learn to love him more!

Intimacy in Worship. I have had some great worship experiences in my car. Of course, I love the opportunities to worship God in a large group setting. It is great to be a part of worship with hundreds of others in a church setting. But sometimes I love to worship God with no one else around.

For one thing, no one else can hear me sing when I am in my car. (Although I do have to be careful during stops at red lights!) I am not musically gifted. I love to sing; it's just that others don't love hearing me sing! I'm not sure if it is the lack of rhythm or the off-key pitch that bothers them most. Whatever the case may be, I can sing my heart out without fear of intimidation or intimidating while in the car.

Worship is, I'm convinced, a private matter that can be done publicly. That is, I can only worship God personally. It is from my heart to the heart of God. But I can also worship God in the presence of others.

The angels broke into praise at the announcement of Jesus' birth. They declared God's glory in the Temple in Isaiah's vision. The book of Revelation records their praises multiple times. Maybe praise is a big deal in heaven. Maybe it should be a bigger deal for us on earth.

I preached recently in a predominately African-American church. The praise and worship was incredible! The congregation sang with such abandon and enthusiasm that I marveled. I am more inhibited. (The first word I spoke as a child was not "Da-da" or "Mama," it was "conservative.") I tend to be cautious in my praise and careful in my worship. But, I must admit, the expressiveness of that worship experience was powerful. I concluded a heavy dose of heartfelt, soul-stirring worship of God was good, right and proper.

Our worship must never become dull and routine. After

all, we are worshiping the God who made the universe, sent his Son to die for our sins, and will return to claim his own. Surely our worship must be more than a meaningless ritual designed to kill an hour or two on Sunday morning!

My wife and I grew up in the Midwest. It's prairie land. There are no mountains (unless you count the interstate overpasses!). Then we moved to Texas. We lived in the Dallas-Fort Worth area. Again, there are no mountains (unless you count the fire ant hills!)

Now, I had gone to the mountains a couple of times while growing up for family vacations and a couple of ski trips. But Vickie had never seen the mountains. So when we were offered a ski trip by a benevolent church member, she was ecstatic! Oh sure, Vickie had seen mountains on post cards and television. But when we flew into Colorado Springs and saw those monstrous peaks, she was totally unprepared. We drove through that beautiful scenery for the next couple of hours while heading for the ski resort. All the way Vickie gasped as she took in the breathtaking sites.

Some of us have seen little postcards of worship. We think we know what worship looks like. But when we truly experience the presence and the breathtaking power of God, our worship takes on new dimensions. We are no longer satisfied with the two-dimensional when we have walked the mountain.

Get alone with God. Reflect on his blessings. Remember again his great love for you. Praise him for his goodness, his mercy, his grace. Gather with the saints and sing his praises together. From your heart to God's heart, let your worship be real and alive. Experience God's presence and glory in his closeness to you!

Intimacy and Revival

When God touches the hearts of his people in revival, their spiritual intimacy with him is deepened. Revival is about God's people growing closer to him. My personal experience with revival has drawn me into a stronger relationship with the

Lord. Studying the nature of revival reminds us of the connection between revival and spiritual intimacy. Certainly we can see this connection as we examine some of the great revival times in history.

One of the most enjoyable and fascinating studies of my seminary days was the study of spiritual awakenings. Unfortunately, our understanding of what revival is all about can be terribly confused. God desires his people to live in a state of revival. But far too often our tendency is to drift into a routine of spiritually connected activity with little spiritual vitality. That is why revival is needed.

The Nature of Revival. When I speak of revival, I am not talking about a series of church meetings. These revival meetings can be wonderful tools and may lead to revival, but revival is more than a series of meetings. Otherwise, a person might find himself or herself saying the contradictory statement, "We had a revival, but no one was revived!"

Also, revival is not evangelism. Evangelism is a natural result of revival, but not revival itself. Revival is for those who are believers already. It is the Christian community that needs revival. The resulting impact of a revival among Christians always includes evangelism of the lost world. But understand that revival must happen to those who are already made alive in Christ.

Many have given definitions of revival. One of the best is by J. Edwin Orr, the great historian of revival. Orr preferred to use the term spiritual awakening instead of revival. So many confused revival with a revival meeting that he began to use a different term. He defined a spiritual awakening as follows:

> *"An Evangelical Awakening is a movement of the Holy Spirit bringing about a revival of New Testament Christianity in the Church of Christ and in its related community. Such an awakening may change in a significant way an individual only; or it may affect a larger group of believers; or it may move a congregation, or the churches of a city or district, or the whole body of believ-*

ers throughout a country or a continent; or indeed the larger body of believers throughout the world. The outpouring of the Spirit effects the reviving of the Church, the awakening of the masses, and the movement of uninstructed peoples towards the Christian faith; the revived Church, by many or by few, is moved to engage in evangelism, in teaching, and in social action."[5]

One of my favorite professors in seminary was (and still is) Dr. Roy Fish. He taught evangelism at Southwestern Baptist Seminary in Fort Worth, Texas, for years. He had a great love for the study and practice of revival and passed that love on to many of his students. His definition of revival is as follows:

"Revival is a fresh touch from God, releasing his people unto fullness of blessing. It is a divine invasion of love, joy, peace, and conviction. It is an outpouring of the Holy Spirit on the church, empowering believers to love each other unconditionally, to rejoice plentifully, to praise God appropriately, to serve him productively, to live lives that are godly, and to witness for him convincingly."[6]

Both of these definitions emphasize the renewal of a close, personal, intimate relationship between the believer and God. There can be no revival without intimacy. It defies the definition. And, trust me, you don't want to go around defying definitions!

The church in the United States has had several wonderful times of revival. Sadly, it seems most believers in America know very little of this great heritage. There have been four major movements of revival times in the United States and several more regional or specialized revival times.[7]

The First Great Awakening began in the American colonies in approximately 1726 and lasted for perhaps thirty years.[8] Leaders such as George Whitefield, Jonathan Edwards and Gilbert Tennent were influential in the spread of the awakening. Churches throughout the region grew rapidly. For example, the number of Baptist churches in New England increased from twenty-one in 1740 to 266 some fifty years later, an increase of well over one thousand percent![9] The strength of the church in American life grew immensely during this time of revival.

Another revival time has been labeled the Second Great Awakening. Lasting from around 1787 until the mid-1840s,[10] this revival time was extraordinarily influential on religious, moral and cultural America.[11] There were three distinct phases of the revival. The first phase took place in the eastern states and greatly impacted the colleges. A second phase was the boisterous, vibrant and, in my opinion, occasionally excessive camp meetings of the frontier (the frontier at that time was in places like Kentucky and Ohio). The third phase included the ministry of Charles G. Finney, who revolutionized church life through his use of "new measures" and his writing, especially *Lectures on Revivals of Religion.* This long period of revival greatly affected the nation and was, I believe, as significant as any event in American religious history.

Possibly the least known, but most fascinating, revival in America is the Awakening of 1857-58. J. Edwin Orr called it "the most thorough and most wholesome (revival) ever known in the Christian church."[12] Sometimes called the "prayer revival," this revival began in New York City as a prayer meeting. Soon, prayer meetings began all over the country with large numbers of conversions following. After thorough research, Orr estimated one million people (out of population of thirty million Americans) made professions of faith during the brief revival time.

A fourth revival time in American history was the Awakening of 1904-08. This worldwide revival was described by Orr as "the most extensive Evangelical Awakening of all time."[13] The Welsh Revival of 1904, with leaders like Evan Roberts, marked the beginning of this revival. But soon the revival spread around the world and to the United States. Influential in the establishment of many schools and mission endeavors, the revival led to great evangelistic results. Estimates of five million conversions around the world during the two greatest years of revival come out of Orr's research.

There have been many other revival times in America, on

a more limited scale. In more recent history, thousands of young people were influenced through the Jesus Movement in the 1970s. Promise Keepers helped thousands of men draw closer to Christ. Campus revivals shook many colleges in 1995. Many local churches and regions have been a part of spiritual awakening.

The Personal Impact of Revival. Ultimately, revival happens one heart at a time. Though thousands may be stirred at the same time, God does his work in each individual. Just as salvation is personal and individual, so revival is personal and individual. God changes our apathy into vibrancy, one believer at a time, when revival comes to our heart.

When revival came in 1995 to our church in Corinth, Texas, many of us took a quantum leap forward in our spiritual lives. We confessed sins. We made relationships with each other right. We got serious about service to the Lord. But most of all, we grew closer to God. The confession, the restoration and the recommitments were all results of the really important part—getting closer to God.

Have you drifted from closeness with Christ? Has your spiritual life become dry and dreary? Healthy leaders recognize the importance of developing closeness with God. It's not enough just to work for God. He wants you to know him. Christian leaders who understand the principles of healthy leadership know the importance of staying close to the source of health.

CHAPTER TWO

DISCOVER A VISION OF
WHAT COULD BE

*Healthy Christian leaders have a clear vision of what God
wants to do through them in ministry.*

Baseball players need really good vision. There's something about a hard object, whizzing through the air at one hundred
miles per hour, which makes good eyesight very helpful. Good
vision is extremely advantageous when trying to hit a fast-mov-
ing round sphere with an elongated and rounded piece of wood.
Batters have to be able to determine the spin of the ball, the veloc-
ity of the delivery and the location of the pitch in relation to home
plate. They must do this while ready to get out of the path should
a wayward fastball imperil their skull! And all of this takes place
in a split-second.

I am in baseball territory. I live and pastor in the St.
Louis suburbs. It's just a short drive across the Mississippi River
to Busch Stadium, land of the former Home Run King. Folks
around here, and all over the country, went kind of crazy when
Mark McGwire broke the single-season home run record of
Roger Maris. (It wasn't a long trip to crazy for some of us!) But
McGwire needed help to do what he did. His natural eyesight is
poor. Without his contact lenses, McGwire is just another big guy
who makes you nervous in dark alleys. You have to *see* the ball
to hit the ball.

Vision is not the only necessary ingredient to being a
good baseball hitter. It is possible to have good eyesight and poor
hand-to-eye coordination or to have a deathly fear of the ball. But
vision is an indispensable ingredient. A good sense of smell can-

not make up for lack of vision. Great hearing can't produce a .300 hitter. And if the sense of taste becomes involved, well, let's just pray it was an off-speed pitch!

In a similar way, vision is indispensable for truly healthy leadership. Like spiritual intimacy, vision isn't the only talent needed for successful church leadership, but it is necessary. When I speak of vision, however, I am not talking only about how things look now. I am talking about how things could look. The question for ministry leaders is "What will this ministry look like if it is everything God wants it to be?" Certainly vision involves the current conditions. But spiritual vision sees what is and what could be.

When I am looking for new staff members to join our ministry team, I want to know their vision. "What will your ministry area look like when you get where you are going?" I ask. "What is your view of the future of this ministry?"

To my mind, vision and faith are inseparable. Faith is what produces vision. Vision is faith applied. We cannot dream great dreams for God without having great faith in God. After all, it is God who accomplishes the work. Vision is not based in our talents but God's talents. It is not our ability that determines vision but God's ability. God is the one who builds great churches and ministries. We are merely the instruments he uses.

God so loves it when we live by faith. Jim Cymbala reminds us of the importance of faith when he says,

> *Without faith, says* Hebrews 11:6, *it is impossible to please God. Nothing else counts if faith is missing. There is no other foundation for Christian living, no matter the amount of self-effort or energy spent. Nothing else touches the Father's heart as much as when his children simply trust him wholeheartedly.*
> *If you lack a vision for ministry, the real problem could be a lack of faith in God.*[14]

You may say, "I can't expect God to do something great through me in this ministry. I'm not very gifted. I don't have much training. The people I work with are stubborn and lazy." The issue is not your strength or ability. It is not the willingness of coworkers to be diligent. The real issue is, "Is God able?"

There is an old story I heard years ago. R. G. Lee was the pastor of Bellevue Baptist Church in Memphis, then (and now) one of the largest churches in the Southern Baptist Convention. It was during the heart of the depression. Money was scarce, and people were nervous. The deacons of that church, the story goes, were gathered to discuss the future of Bellevue. The church had built a new building and owed money. The men worried they might not be able to pay the bills. Maybe the church would go under. Maybe they wouldn't make it. Maybe they should "hunker down," as they used to say in the South.

Lee listened to all he could stand. His reputation was as a man who spoke his mind. He stood to his feet, it is said, and spoke to the deacons, "Men, I've been listening to you talk and I want to ask you a question. When did God die?"

"What do you mean?" they asked incredulously.

"You are talking as though God is dead." Lee stated. "My Father owns the cattle on a thousand hills and he will supply all our needs as we live by faith and do his will."

That speech, apocryphal or not, is the kind of speech churches and ministries need to hear today. Either God is able to do what he says or he is not. If we believe he is able, how can we hold to small dreams and puny plans? Our vision of the future is determined by our faith in the God who holds the future.

I am constantly amazed at the kind of people God uses. I keep expecting God to use the superstar. Sometimes he does. But often I discover these Christian "superstars" are much like the rest of us. They have weaknesses and frailties too. And yet God uses them because he is the one who does the work anyway. We are the instruments, God is the power.

Often, God seems to do his best work through people who aren't superstars. He uses very ordinary people to do his extraordinary work. These people are neither famous nor unusually talented. They seem downright ordinary. But God displays his extraordinary power through them.

Occasionally, God uses people I would not choose. They are stubborn and ornery, and God works through their lives anyway. Sometimes their motives seem less than pure, but God blesses through them anyway. God uses people who stutter and mangle prepositions to proclaim his word. He uses people with reading disorders to teach faithfully. I have even witnessed God using people who are "halitosis-challenged" (that means they have bad breath) to testify of his grace.

Yes, we ought to do God's work with proper motives and attitudes. Yes, we should do our best to study, learn and train. And, yes, by all means remember to use breath mints! But we dare not forget that God is able to use us to accomplish his purposes despite our frailties. After all, it is God that makes any lasting changes anyway. God uses ordinary people to accomplish extraordinary results.

The Power of a Goal

A few years ago I ran a marathon. (It would be more apt to say I was run over by a marathon!) A marathon is 26.2 miles. And let me tell you, after 26 miles the .2 counts. It was the most exhausting thing I have ever done. (And I have shopped with my wife!)

I ran the marathon with Chuck, one of my friends from church, and Dan, one of my brothers who is also a medical doctor. (Let me recommend to those of you considering a first marathon that you run with a doctor who is fully up to date on CPR training!) When we started the race, after 18 weeks of serious training, we were in a jovial mood. We laughed; we joked; we had a good time. By mile 20 the humor was gone. We were praying for survival. All I could think about was food and heart failure. Not necessarily in that order.

At about mile 25, an interesting thing happened as Dan and I ran together. Dan is 8 years younger than me but shared my exhaustion that day. Along the course, there are spectators who gather to encourage the runners. They say things like, "Good job!" "Keep it up!" "Someone call a paramedic!" Well, Dan and I were running along (perhaps the word "staggering" is more accurate) when a young adult lady called out, "Look! A father and son running together!" And suddenly I realized she thought I was the father!

I looked over at my brother. He was 31 at the time, but the wear and the tear of the race had taken its toll. He was covered with sweat and was drooling. His eyes were sunken and glazed. His face was pale; his cheeks were sunken; his breathing erratic. He gave every appearance of a man twice his age coming off a week-long drinking binge. And the lady thought I was his father. His *father* for crying out loud! "How bad must I look," I thought "if she thinks I am this guy's father!"

Now why does an otherwise (somewhat) normal guy go out and abuse himself in such a fashion? What motivates a fellow to endure the effort and hard work of training for 18 weeks and running for much of a day? The answer is simple. I set a goal.

When I was in college, I announced to several of my buddies that I had three goals I wanted to accomplish. I wanted to run a marathon, write a book and not get fat. (I think this is a good time to say "Two out of three isn't bad.") These were just a couple of things I wanted to accomplish in my life. (Really, I was just kidding about the not getting fat thing. That one was just a joke.) So I said this to some friends. Out loud.

At a class reunion a few years back, I was reminiscing with an old friend when he brought up the old goals. "What about that marathon?" he wanted to know. "Why haven't you run one?" Goals can be powerful things.

I didn't run a marathon because I enjoy running. I know some of you love to run. That's great. I think you are sick, but that's great. I didn't run to improve my health or impress my wife or win a race. (Though I did lose the race by only two hours or so!) I ran the marathon because I set a goal. And goals can be powerful.

Visionaries and Dreamers. There is a difference between visionaries and dreamers. Visionaries are people who see things as they could be and work to see those things accomplished. Dreamers are people who see things as they wish they were but are not willing to make the effort to accomplish them. I have met more dreamers in my life than visionaries.

Don't think vision is dreaming about how nice it will be if your ministry flourishes. Vision is seeing what really can be. It is not an unattainable wish. It is not fruitless imagination. It is believing God can use you, with all your frailties and weaknesses, to do something great for his glory. And it always leads to action. The Bible reminds us, "faith by itself, if it is not accompanied by action, is dead." (James 2:17)

Many people dream. It's safe, it's easy, and it's cheap. But having vision is risky. It requires effort, maybe even sacrifice. (And often hard work!) Failure is a possibility. But, oh, how exciting to believe God for great things and to accomplish the "impossible" for his glory. Visionaries are always thinking about ways to reach their dreams.

Benefits of Goals. Having a goal can help the leader in several ways. First of all, a goal can help you see where you are. The first step to finding out where you are going is to discover where you are. In our local mall are directional maps. They tell you where the stores are located (and more importantly, the location of the food court). And always there is a big red arrow that points to a spot on the map and says "You are here." (I like it when the arrow is near the food court.)

I like that arrow. I need to know where I am in order to know how to get where I want to go. (Usually, I want to go to the food court.) But I am amazed at how many people don't know seem to know where they are. They wander aimlessly through life without any real purpose. They never check the arrow to see where they are. A goal helps you focus on your present condition, which in turn, helps you to get where you need to be. It helps you to see what you have not done so that you can do what needs to be done.

A second benefit of a goal is that it helps you to see the possibilities. Goal setting forces you to examine what might be. A goal says your potential is greater than your present conditions. It focuses on something greater in the future.

I have a story I tell every year at our church. It's about

food courts. Just kidding! It's about Abraham Lincoln. Whether it is true or not, I do not know. But it is certainly "Lincoln-like." It is said that President Lincoln was invited by a friend to attend a particular church in Washington, D. C. The friend told him about the marvelous speaking ability of the pastor of the church and suggested Lincoln would enjoy the services. So, Lincoln attended one Sunday morning. He listened as the preacher spoke eloquently about his subject. After the service concluded, the friend asked the president how he liked the sermon. Lincoln paused, so the man pressed the issue. Lincoln reportedly said that the preacher was obviously a gifted communicator. He was very skilled as an orator. But Lincoln said he didn't really like the sermon that much. "Why not?" his friend asked. "Because," Lincoln stated, "he didn't ask me to do anything great."

This story reminds us that God asks us to do something great. The reason we set goals is because a great God asks us to do great things. Goals remind us that we have potential that we have not yet accomplished. Goals help us see the possibilities.

In 1995, on my first Sunday as the new pastor of First Baptist Church of O'Fallon, I told that Lincoln story. I told them I believed we could average 1,000 people in Sunday school by the year 2000. That goal seemed huge then. (The church had averaged exactly 564 people in Sunday school for the previous two consecutive years.) But it opened our eyes to the possibilities. And by God's grace we reached and exceeded that goal. Setting the goal opened our eyes to where we were and where we could be. And it helped us to do more than we might otherwise have done.

A third benefit of a goal is that it helps you focus on the essentials. I am easily distracted. If I go out to eat at a restaurant that has televisions, I have to sit facing away from the screen-especially if some sporting event is on the tube. Otherwise, bad things can happen. For instance, my wife and I may be eating out, and she begins to talk about something really important. But then I notice some action in a ballgame on the television set. So, instead of listening to her I am focused on some game that has no real relevance to me. She tends to not like that very much.

Goals help us stay focused on the essentials instead of the peripheral issues. By nature, they cause us to think about priorities and steer us toward the essentials. We are less likely to follow the distractions that constantly spring up in ministry.

A fourth benefit of a goal is that it leads you toward effectiveness, not just activity. My daughter, Rachel, has a pet hamster. It's kind of a hairy mouse with a short tail. She named her hamster Pinkie. Pinkie the hamster has a little cage with wood chips, a water bottle and food bowl. And, of course, no hamster cage is complete without a running wheel! Pinkie loves to get in that wheel and run. He will run for hours at a time. And Pinkie, being a hamster, is nocturnal by nature. He loves to get in that wheel about midnight and go on a nice jog. Often, late at night I can hear the faint squeak of the wheel. Pinkie is on the move.

There is only one problem. Pinkie never gets anywhere. No matter how much activity, Pinkie never leaves the cage. Many people confuse activity for effectiveness. The question isn't how much work you do, but how effective you are.

Peter Wagner told the story of a pastor who tried to evangelize his community by knocking on doors house-by-house, street-by-street. He and his team knocked on 4,000 doors. "How many converts did you get?" he was asked. "None," he replied. His friend asked, "What are you going to do now?" He answered, "We're going to redouble our efforts and call on 8,000 homes this next year!"[15] Lots of activity, little effectiveness.

Rick Warren notes in his book, *The Purpose Driven Church*, the importance of effectiveness and not just activity. Some people suggest God desires only faithfulness, not effectiveness. Warren states,

> *"God wants your church to be both faithful and fruitful. One without the other is only half the equation. Numerical results are no justification for being unfaithful to the message, but neither can we use faithfulness as an excuse for being ineffective! Churches that have few or no conversions often attempt to justify their ineffectiveness with the statement, 'God has not called us to be successful. He has just called us to be faithful.' I strongly*

disagree because the Bible clearly teaches that God expects both."[16]

When you confuse activity for effectiveness, you can easily run harder without any progress. You may have the best intentions, but little is actually accomplished. Setting the right goals can help you avoid that mistake.

Reaching any large goal is the result of setting and attaining lots of smaller goals along the way. A large goal focuses attention on the big picture. It helps us see what can be done. But smaller goals help us with realism. They show us that step-by- step the larger goal can be accomplished.

Understanding that setting and reaching smaller goals is the key to reaching larger ones is often the difference between visionaries and dreamers. Great goals are rarely accomplished overnight. They are most often the result of taking a series of smaller steps. I could run a marathon because I accomplished shorter but progressively longer runs over a period of weeks. My big goal was 26.2 miles. The goal for my first day of training was 3 miles. If I had set a goal of a 3 mile run, I could have accomplished it without any other goals. But to reach a big goal I needed to reach a series of smaller goals. So for eighteen weeks I set and reached a series of goals that led to my ultimate goal of running a marathon (and living to tell about it).

The relationship of small and large goals is important. I would not have run all the shorter runs had it not been for the looming marathon. The big goal, and my desire to survive it, was the motivation to accomplish the small goals. The small goals enabled me to accomplish the big goal.

After setting a goal of 1,000 people in Sunday School by the year 2000, our church family adopted several smaller goals that helped us reach the larger goal. We had special one-Sunday-goals. Each age group set individual goals for their area. These smaller targets helped us accomplish larger objectives.

Dreamers picture a big goal. They just fail to take the series of smaller steps that are necessary to accomplish the dream. Those who lack vision may see small goals. But they never get sight of the big goal that serves to motivate and navigate them.

Learning to Prioritize. One of the most important parts of setting goals and reaching visions is learning to prioritize. But it can be a hard lesson to learn. So many different items clamor for attention. So many issues will vie for your time and energy. The key to accomplishing your visions is prioritizing those items and issues that matter most.

I have had many times when my priorities got out of line. I sometimes get so busy with details I loose sight of what matters most. At times, I pay lip service to my priorities but don't live them out. Sometimes, it's just difficult for me to see what really matters.

Many people, even those who love Jesus, struggle with finding and following the right priorities. There are four questions that can help believers discover and follow their priorities.

Question One: What are my goals? Have I articulated my goals? What matters most to me? One reason many people struggle with doing great things is that they have never considered what great things they ought to do. They have not marked out their goals or targets.

I like to hunt with bow and arrows. It seems so primitive, so difficult, so manly. Nothing says manhood like some beef jerky (let the juice trickle down the corner of your mouth for the full effect), a dirty baseball cap, some good scratching and shooting a bow and arrow.

Learning to shoot accurately takes practice so when I have the opportunity, I drag out my compound bow, my arrows and my target. My target is just a big square bag made of tough, durable material. It has a series of concentric circles that lead to the bulls-eye. Whenever I practice, I try to aim for the center of the bulls-eye. I know exactly what my goal is: to hit the center of the target.

Now imagine for a moment that I decide to use a different strategy. Imagine I shoot the arrows at random then draw a bulls-eye around the place where the arrow lands. Boy, would that lookgood! My shooting would tend to look a whole lot better if I did things that way. But would my shooting actually be better if I had no goal to shoot for?

A lot of Christian leaders do something like that. Without a clear target they are never quite sure where to aim. They may even start to confuse results with goals. Wherever they land in life, they draw a target and say they are on the mark. But often they lack the effectiveness that comes with setting a real goal and making that a priority.

The problem with setting a definable goal is that you might miss. Trust me. I know about missing targets. Hunting for errant arrows has become something of a habit. But I also know that shooting for a real goal is the best way to reach that goal.

Do you have some clear, well-defined goals in your life? Can you name them, touch them, feel them? If a friend or relative were asked to name your goals, could they come close? Far too many live their lives with no sense of priorities because they have never stopped to consider the benefits of goals. Or maybe they didn't want to risk failure. Or maybe they just never took the time.

Mull over a minute what your goals really are. Perhaps this would be a good time to write them down. When you get right down to it, what are the bulls-eyes of your ministry? What are the targets you are aiming at in life?

Question Two: What if I reach my goals? A second part of setting the right priorities is to consider what it would be like to reach those goals you have set. Once you get where you are going will you be glad you are there?

Oh I looked forward to the moment! I could just picture it in my mind! The joy, the fun, the challenge. It was enough to send my twelve-year-old mind into adolescent nirvana!

What, you ask, was I so excited about? Why the great Rainbow Lodge, of course. We had seen billboards miles before. They promised ten thousand rainbow trout (not just any trout, mind you, but *rainbow* trout) in their picturesque lake. We were on a family vacation in the mountains of Colorado. My parents, somewhat uncharacteristically, had not arranged for lodging for the night's stay. So when I saw the billboards advertising ten thousand rainbow trout in a picturesque lake, I knew the Rainbow Lodge was the place for me.

With some pleading and promises never to fight with my three brothers again (I am pretty sure I broke that promise), my parents finally agreed to stop at this impressive resort. And so, mile after mile, I waited. Once in a while we saw another billboard. I could picture the battle of wits between boy and trout. I would fool them with my superior cranial capacity. The anticipation nearly killed me!

As we drew closer, the excitement grew more intense. I overlooked my obnoxious brothers. (I was always amazed at how obnoxious my brothers could be while I was always so thoughtful and caring.) I had a goal in mind and soon those trout would be matched against the greatest young angler in North America.

When we arrived at Rainbow Lodge, I immediately headed for the lake stocked with ten thousand rainbow trout. But the only thing I could see was just a little pond. I asked a man working there where the lake filled with ten thousand rainbow trout was. He said the pond was it.

I looked into the small pond and found it stuffed with fish. They were packed in like sardines. And I didn't want sardines, I wanted rainbow trout! I dropped in a piece of grass. Hundreds of fish went after it in a frenzy of whitewater. The bait the fishermen used wasn't some beautifully hand-crafted lure. It was a piece of corn on a hook. The bait was taken the moment it touched the water. This wasn't fishing. The poor, hungry fish didn't have a chance. But I had reached the goal I had longed to reach for miles.

"I got the corner office. I made lots of money. All my goals were reached," a businessman once told me. "But I was as hollow after I reached them as I had been before I started."

Are you headed for the right goals? What if you reach the goals for which you are headed? Will you be glad you got there? Be certain you are headed toward goals that you really want to attain. Otherwise, be ready for a pond full of disappointment.

Question Three: Have I prioritized the best over the good? I couldn't decide what to do. Should I spend some quality time with the family or should I knock off a Savings and Loan? It was a tough decision.

No, that isn't how prioritizing tends to work. We don't tend to decide between the worst and the best. We tend to decide between the good and the best. I don't choose between robbing banks and quality family time. I decide between television and quality family time. It isn't that watching television is bad. It can be a good thing in moderation. But often I choose good things instead of the best things.

The greatest enemy of excellence is not incompetence. The greatest enemy of excellence is mediocrity. Far too many church leaders have settled for good things instead of God's best for their lives. Far too many churches and Christian organizations have prioritized the good over the best.

Setting the right priorities is not just about avoiding bad things. It is also about being actively involved with the right things. Don't settle for good priorities. Reach for the best. John Maxwell made this point when he said,

> *Most people can prioritize when faced with right or wrong issues. The challenge arises when we are faced with two good choices. Now what should we do? What if both choices fall comfortably into the requirement, return, and reward of our work?*[17]

Finding God's best for your life is one of the most important responsibilities you face. There are many good things you can do in life. But finding the best thing is the key. Spend time in prayer asking God to show you his best for your life. Talk with godly friends and family to get their perspective. Consider your gifts and passions. Take advantage of opportunities to test your abilities and aptitude.

During my college years I was looking for my place in life. I considered several career possibilities. I liked sports. I thought I might coach. I liked money. I thought I might become a high-powered attorney. But more than anything, I wanted to find God's best for my life and career.

I prayed many times, asking God to show me his plan for my future. I told God I was open to whatever he wanted in my life. I wanted to follow his plan for my life whatever that might be. (I secretly hoped his plan involved me becoming a professional athlete.) The answer was not what I expected.

The summer after my sophomore year of college, my home church was without a Youth and Children's minister. They wanted to know if I would be interested in being an interim for the summer. I needed a job and, while this didn't seem to be my cup of tea, I thought, "Why not?" They paid me a little and gave me an office and told me, "Good luck!" I ran the church's large bus ministry that went through the region picking up children for Sunday school. I "preached" the children's message for the kids and planned the children's worship service. I planned and promoted some youth activities. And I loved it.

By the end of that summer I knew God wanted me in some sort of vocational ministry. I didn't know all of what that meant. I certainly didn't know at that time I would become a pastor. But it became so clear that this was God's best for my life.

I could have been a good coach. But that wasn't God's best for me. I might have been a wealthy attorney. But that wasn't God's best for me. And choosing the best over the good is the key to having the correct priorities.

Question Four: Are my goals Kingdom goals? When my son was six years old he informed me that he wanted to be a super hero when he grows up. He planned on being a scientist who builds a special suit that can help him "fight bad guys." He had it all planned out. He even started working with some possible nicknames and potential sidekicks. (You've got to have nicknames and sidekicks to be a superhero.)

That's a pretty neat goal, I guess. Not too realistic, perhaps, but neat nonetheless. I mean, fighting bad guys and all, well . . . someone has to do it. Come to think of it, that's something I am supposed to do. The Bible describes us as fighting a battle. And our battle is big! "For our struggle is not against flesh and blood, but against the rulers, against the authorities, against the powers of this dark world and against the spiritual forces of evil in the heavenly realms." (Ephesians 6:12)

It is part of a kingdom-sized goal to be involved in spiritual warfare. And God certainly has some kingdom goals for us. A beautiful reminder of that is found in Jeremiah 29: 11. It says, "'For I know the plans I have for you,' declares the Lord, 'plans to prosper you and not to harm you, plans to give you hope and a future.'" God has plans for us. And they are good! They are designed by God to give us hope and a future. They are kingdom plans.

Ephesians 2:10 echoes that same thought. "For we are God's workmanship, created in Christ Jesus to do good works, which God prepared in advance for us to do." Before we were ever saved, God made plans for us. They are kingdom plans.

God has plans and goals for us. We are to be a part of his work in the world. Our goals should be more than just earthly goals or personal goals. They should be kingdom goals!

Wise is the person who sets goals for God's kingdom and not for self. One day we are going to stand before God. That day may be decades away, but from the perspective of eternity, it is just a moment away. What we have done for self will fade away. What we do for God's kingdom and glory will last.

Joseph Stowell, in his excellent book Eternity, told this story about golfer Paul Azinger that puts it in perspective.

> *Paul Azinger was at the height of his professional golf career when the doctor told him that he had life-threatening cancer. Up to that moment he had not given much thought to dying. Life was too all-consuming for him to stop and consider the reality of the grave and all that is beyond. But that encounter with the inevitability of eternity was an abrupt reality check. His life would never again be the same. Even the $1.46 million he had made as a professional golfer that year paled to insignificance. All he could think about was what the chaplain of the tour had said: "We think that we are in the land of the living going to the land of the dying when in reality we are in the land of the dying headed for the land of the living."*[18]

I love cemeteries. I know that sounds weird, but I do. Having conducted many funerals, cemeteries do not hold the fear of the unknown for me. They are not just a place of death for me. They are a place for stories and memories. They remind us of the stories of life. The memories of the past are relived there. But cemeteries also remind us that we are mortal. One day, should the Lord tarry, my body will be laid in a grave, and I will face eternity. That is a good reminder to me that I need to live my life with eternity in mind.

I determined to make all of my important decisions in a cemetery. All major decisions in my life are made right there among the grave markers. It is a tangible reminder to me of the brevity of my life. It reminds me to make those decisions in light of eternity. It reminds me to be certain to follow kingdom goals rather than merely personal goals.

Leaders with Leadership health have vision. They see what God can do. They believe a great God for great things. They believe God is capable of using them, with all their frailties, to accomplish his purposes.

Have you had your vision checked lately? Are you seeing your world as it is and as it could be? Have you asked God to show you what could be? If not, the Great Physician is very capable as an Optometrist, and he is happy to make house calls still today!

CHAPTER THREE

DEVELOP A PASSION
FOR REACHING PEOPLE

*Healthy Christian Leaders are passionate about reaching
people for Christ and teaching them to follow him as Lord.*

I woke up the other night dreaming about deer. Not my
dear wife; deer as in the animal. You see, I started deer hunting a
few years ago and I have gotten rather interested in it. I use a bow
and arrows for my hunting as it seems more sporting. It is merely coincidental, of course, that the bow hunting season is signifi-
cantly longer, allowing me to hunt far more frequently than otherwise would be possible. Merely coincidental. So now I practice shooting my bow and arrows. I read magazines and books
about how to hunt more effectively. I buy equipment that is supposed to make me blend into the woods, or eliminate my smell,
or add to my comfort, or break my bank account. For crying out
loud, I even dream about deer. I think my wife may be getting a
little upset. Obviously, I have a passion for deer hunting.

I watch sports on television. Lots of sports. I watch all
of the major American sports like football, baseball, basketball,
hockey, tennis, golf, track and field, gymnastics, soccer, bowling,
skiing, skateboarding, surfing, volleyball, cycling, boxing, bad-
minton, yard darts and the like. I even watch some of the inter-
national sports like Australian club league rugby and sumo
wrestling. (I do want to note for the record that I have never
dreamed of sumo wrestling!) I have sat in freezing cold nights
and ridiculously hot days to watch sports events. I scream at the
television, ranting about officials and calling out unheard encouragement to my team. My interest level is that high. Obviously, I
have a passion for sports.

It is amazing how passionate I can be about things that have little lasting value. Nothing wrong with having hobbies, of course, but they aren't on the same level of importance as eternal matters. My real point is not that we are too passionate about our interests and hobbies, true as that may be, but that we have too little passion about spiritual matters and people created in God's image.

One of the key ingredients in people who are effective is passion. Successful musicians have a passion for their music. Successful business leaders are passionate about their job. Successful parents are passionate about their responsibilities to their children. That passion is obvious in what they do and the choices they make.

Yet, many churches and Christian organizations seem to lose their passion for reaching people. Normally, churches begin with a real commitment to reach people. They have a passion to grow. Perhaps that explains why new church starts are frequently more effective in reaching people than established churches. But often churches that began with a strong emphasis on reaching people lose their zeal. Their passions turn to programs, buildings and budgets and they lose passion for seeing lives changed by the power of the gospel. They are not necessarily against church growth; they just don't have the same enthusiasm for the task they once had. Christian organizations that once existed to impact the lives of people can sometimes exist to continue to exist. The concern for touching lives can turn to concern for institutional survival.

The Bible says, "Never be lacking in zeal, but keep your spiritual fervor, serving in the Lord." (Romans 12:11) God gives these words to remind us of the danger of "lacking in zeal". We can lose our "spiritual fervor". Our passion for serving the Lord needs to be kept alive and vibrant. It is easy for a person or an organization to lose that zeal. The passion for doing God's work is like a flame that needs to be fanned and fed or it will weaken and be extinguished.

The church at Ephesus was passionate about serving the Lord. But over time that passion waned. Eventually, Jesus said of them, "You have forsaken your first love." (Rev. 2:4) Without care, our passion for God's work can be slowly extinguished until it is a smoldering ember instead of a burning flame.

What are you passionate about? The things you treasure give you some clues about your passions. The Bible reminds us, "Where your treasure is, there your heart will be also." (Mt. 6:21) If you treasure security or wealth or fame you will be passionate about those things. But if your treasure is found in serving the Lord and his kingdom you will find a passion in your ministry.

Those who understand healthy leadership are keenly aware of the importance of passionate ministry. Christian leaders need to be passionate, but that zeal should be about the same things God is passionate about. Our concerns need to match his concerns. Our interests should reflect his interests.

God's Passion for People

What is God passionate about? What gets his attention? *God cares passionately about people.* The Bible is full of God's great love and concern for those created in his image. Jesus, the Son of God, demonstrated his great passion for people on many occasions. He touched people, he healed people, he taught people and he died for people.

From the beginning God had a special care and concern for people. Genesis 1 says, "God created man in his own image." He created man for fellowship and he values our lives and potential. He made us for a purpose and has a plan for our lives.

When I consider my life I am amazed that God would care so deeply about me. He is so great and so big; and I am so small and frail. I understand something of how David must have felt when he said, "When I consider your heavens, the work of your fingers, the moon and the stars, which you have set in place, what is man that you are mindful of him, the son of man that you care for him?" (Psalm 8:3-4) Why should God care about little specks like us in this vast universe?

Thankfully, God does care for little specks like us. David continued, "You have made him a little lower than the heavenly beings and crowned him with glory and honor. You made him ruler over the works of your hands; you put everything under his feet." (Psalm 8:5-6) God's great love for people seemed overwhelming to David as he considered the world God made. And yet David recognized how greatly God values our lives.

When Steven Jobs was founding Apple Computers he needed some help. He knew computers inside and out. On the technical side, he excelled. But businesses, especially new businesses about to compete with the likes of IBM, need sound marketing strategies and Jobs needed help. He began a search that led him to John Sculley, the talented, young executive with Pepsi-Cola. Jobs did all he could to convince Sculley to leave Pepsi and come to work with him. He wined him and dined him and made promises he couldn't keep. Nothing seemed to work. After all, who in their right mind would leave the security of Pepsi for some upstart computer company no one knew? But then Jobs is said to have asked a question that changed Sculley's mind. He asked, "Do you want to spend the rest of your life selling sugared water, or do you want a chance to change the world?"

When you are involved with people you are in the world changing business. Loving people in Jesus' name is more than selling sugared water; it's changing lives for eternity. People matter deeply to God and should matter to those who know God. When we are in tune with the heart of God we are passionate about people because God is passionate about people.

Church buildings are great but they are not the goal of church life. Church buildings are a tool, a means to an end, to help us reach and teach people. Church programs are good but they are not the goal of church life. Programs are a means by which we can reach and teach people. Churches and ministries must beware of allowing buildings or programs or other good things to become the focus of their passion. Our zeal is to focus on people because they are objects of God's affection.

God cares passionately about lost people. While it is difficult to imagine that God loves us so deeply at our best, it seems almost impossible that God could love us deeply at our worst. God's passion for sinners is seen clearly in Romans 5:8. "But God demonstrates his own love for us in this: While we were still sinners, Christ died for us." It is obvious from the cross that God cares about sinful men and women and wants them to come back into right relation with him.

This passion for lost people is exemplified many times in the life of Jesus. On several occasions the religious leaders had trouble accepting this passion. The Gospels record how Jesus invited Matthew the tax collector to follow him.[19] The decision to follow Jesus was obviously life changing for Matthew who was willing to leave everything to become a disciple. After meeting Jesus, Matthew held a great banquet for Jesus in his home. As might be expected, Matthew invited his friends to meet this great savior. His friends were tax collectors and other undesirables and Matthew must have been thrilled to see so many gather to meet Christ.

But not everyone was so happy about the meeting. The Pharisees and teachers of the law gathered and complained to the disciples, "Why do you eat and drink with tax collectors and 'sinners'?" They were disgusted with the people they found in Jesus' presence.

Jesus used this occasion to point out his purpose. He reminded all present, "It is not the healthy who need a doctor, but the sick... For I have not come to call the righteous, but sinners." (Mt. 9:12, 13) Jesus deeply loves people and desires that they come to know him as Savior and Lord.

Dan, my doctor brother, sometimes works at the First Aid centers at sporting events. One year he provided medical support at a marathon in Dallas, Texas. The White Rock marathon attracts thousands of marathoners each year in December. Doctors, nurses and other volunteers help with any medical needs that arise. Usually the cases are relatively minor, like blisters and minor dehydration, but there is always the potential for more serious ailments.

Not much was going on at the First Aid tent during this particular race so Dan and an Intern named Ken decided to go to the finish line to watch runners complete their races. Just as they arrived at the finish line, Dan noticed a marathon runner who was staggering. Worried about the man's safety, Dan approached him just as he crossed the finish line. Dan asked, "Sir, are you all right?" The runner mumbled something incoherent and collapsed in Dan's arms. His eyes rolled back in his head and he fainted. Dan laid him on the ground and felt for a pulse. There was no pulse.

Dan and Ken knew this was a serious, possibly fatal emergency. They immediately began CPR and mouth-to-mouth resuscitation. The runner's family, joyfully gathered to celebrate the finish of the marathon, now panicked at the site of a life and death struggle. Some screamed in terror. They cried and begged the doctors to save him. All the while, runners continued to stream into the area of the finish line oblivious to the unfolding drama, stumbling over the doctors frantically working to save a man's life.

An ambulance was called immediately after the runner collapsed, but the huge number of runners and spectators made it difficult for them to get to the finish line. Paramedics were eventually able to get a crash cart to the scene and the doctors ran an IV and intubated the man. Still, there was no heartbeat. The crash cart had a defibrillator and Dan knew what he must do. He had to shock the victim, hoping it would jolt his heart back into action. Knowing the great danger to anyone who might touch the man while he was being shocked, Dan tried to shield others from the victim. He used his foot to block one poor runner who had just struggled to complete the marathon, unaware of the nearby danger. But even volts of electricity did not restart the runner's heart.

Finally, after twenty minutes of CPR, the ambulance arrived. They loaded the runner into the back. Still, there was no heartbeat. Dan and Ken turned the job over to the paramedics and watched as they drove away. Numb from the experience, and knowing the odds were against the fallen man, the two doctors watched the ambulance weave through the crowd to the emergency room. Were all their efforts in vain?

To their surprise and delight, Dan and Ken later learned

that on the way to the hospital the runner's heart began to beat on its own. Jim, a thirty-nine year old husband and father from Indiana, spent three days in ICU and eventually fully recovered. This experienced runner had an undetected heart ailment that can become fatal when one is severely dehydrated. He was at the brink of death and survived. Had he fallen a mile earlier, he almost certainly would have died. Had he not literally fallen into the arms of a doctor who immediately began CPR, his life would likely have ended.

The man and his family were so grateful. They came so close to losing each other, and almost miraculously a family was spared a loss. Jim and his family wrote a gracious letter to Dan thanking him profusely for his help. They poured out their emotions, grateful for his life-saving assistance. It is a letter Dan will always treasure.

Maybe that one life doesn't seem like much to some. But that one man was a husband, a father, a son and a brother. Fear of his death brought despair. The salvation of that life brought rejoicing. That family was thankful for a doctor that was passionate about saving the life of a dying man.

I don't always understand why God loves lost people so much. But I am glad he loved me, a sinner in need of a Savior. I'm glad he saved me when I could do nothing to save myself. I am so thankful he caught me when I fell. God cares passionately about lost people.

God cares passionately about saved people reaching lost people. If God cares so much that lost people come to salvation, what method does he use? What about writing the message of salvation in the clouds? That would be certain to garner some attention. Perhaps transmitting God's voice through the air is a better method. People would surely respond to that. But, surprisingly, God chose to send his message to a lost world through people like us.

II Corinthians 5:17-21 tells believers they have been given the "ministry of reconciliation." Those who have experienced his grace now have the "message of reconciliation." We become "Christ's ambassadors" representing Jesus to lost people in our world. What method does God use to bring people to faith? He uses people who know his love to tell others of his love. I am to represent Christ in this world by pointing others to faith in Jesus. And this responsibility is not for missionaries and pastors alone. All who follow Christ are a part of God's plan for evangelizing the world.

Evangelism, telling others how to know Jesus Christ as Savior and Lord, is frightening to most of us Christians. We fear rejection. We are afraid we will embarrass ourselves or the cause of Christ. The ominous fear of the unknown haunts us. If the subject of sharing your faith causes trepidation, you are not alone. Most of us struggle with evangelistic reluctance. A story is told in II Kings 6 and 7 that encourages me in evangelism.

In the days of the prophet Elisha, a terrible famine gripped the city of Samaria due to a military siege by the Arameans. The siege meant no food got into the city and the Arameans could bide their time and starve the people out. Things got so bad a donkey's head sold for a small fortune and some even resorted to cannibalism.

Outside the city walls were four lepers. They were stuck between a rock and a hard place. They desperately needed food but the city had nothing to offer but slow death. The only other choice was to go to the Arameans and beg for food. It seemed highly unlikely that the Arameans would assist. They would probably kill them. But maybe that death would be swift.

How shocked the lepers were to discover the Aramean camp empty. Not only was it empty, but all their belongings, most importantly their food, was left behind! God provided a miracle. Just prior to the arrival of the lepers, the Arameans heard the sound of an army and fled leaving all their belongings. There was food in abundance. The lepers ate and drank to content and beyond. They began to hide the silver and gold. Then they thought about Samaria.

The people were starving. Food was gone and hope was vanishing. The lepers knew what they must do. The Bible records their conversation. "We're not doing right. This is a day of good news and we are keeping it to ourselves. If we wait until daylight, punishment will overtake us. Let's go at once and report this to the royal palace." (II Kings 7:9) Because of their actions the city was saved.

Evangelism was once defined by D. T. Niles as "one beggar telling another beggar where to get food." [20] Four lepers understood the need and invited others to the feast. God is passionate that beggars like us tell other beggars about the wonderful Bread of Life. I don't have to know all the answers to all the questions. I can tell people where the bread is.

I am glad God allows me to participate in the salvation of people. It is so exciting to participate physically and spiritually in a conversion experience. When our four children were born, I was in the birthing room with my wife. I experienced the incredible moment of joy and fear and relief at their birth. When I am old and senile (my children tell me that moment is not far away), I will still remember the excitement of that moment when that little child was placed in my arms.

God allows me to participate in the new birth of men and women into his kingdom. When I have the privilege of leading someone to Christ it is as though I am in a spiritual birthing room with all the joy and fear and relief. How blessed we are to have the opportunity to participate in such a wonderful experience. God could do all his work without me. I am grateful he often chooses to do his work through me.

Sharing my faith with others is one of the best ways for me to grow spiritually. Lost people sometimes ask me questions which are difficult to answer. That causes me to study and search the scriptures which in turn enlightens and encourages me. Lost people look at my example. That causes me to desire a holy life that bears testimony to my Lord. My obedience to God in evangelism is an important part of my development as a disciple of Jesus. I cannot be all God wants me to be in discipleship without being all God wants me to be in evangelism.

Even God's call to holy living has a connection to his passion for lost people. Ultimately, I am called to be holy because holiness is the nature of God. I am to be like him in character. But a side result of that call to holiness is evangelistic opportunities resulting from my lifestyle. Lifestyle evangelism is the result of people being drawn to God's character by my imitation of it. The integrity of my life draws people to the ultimate giver of integrity.

My passion for lost people reminds me of my responsibility to live an exemplary life. The quality of my life is a testimony of God's grace. My service to others, my sacrifice of self, my kindness to enemies, all these things reflect the Lord's nature. If I truly love lost people I desire to show them the life-changing power of God.

Healthy Christian leaders are passionate about lost people because they recognize God's passion for lost people. Their actions and attitudes reflect that recognition.

Passion and Priorities

Christian leaders who accomplish much for God are people of great passion. One of the reasons is because passion causes them to focus their attention and energy on the things that matter most. Passionate people focus on essentials.

Passionate people set priorities because they recognize the shortness of time. A story is told of a little boy who made a Father's Day card for his dad. He wrote these words to his father. "Dear Dad, I love you and hope you live all your life." Life is too short not to live it all. It is just a moment in the scope of eternity.

I was in a speaking at a conference in Vandalia, Illinois some time ago. The town is rather old by Illinois standards and once served as the capital of the state. I had some time one afternoon and decided to visit one of the local cemeteries to see some of the old grave markers which often reveal interesting stories. One of the grave markers in particular caught my attention. It was the grave of a remarkable Civil War Colonel named Lucien Greathouse.

Greathouse was born in the central Illinois town of

Carlinville. He joined the northern forces when hostilities broke out between the states. Throughout his distinguished career Greathouse was involved in many armed conflicts. His grave stone notes that he "led his command in forty pitched battles." He was at Vicksburg during the siege of that strategic city. He marched south toward Atlanta with the Union troops (called somewhat confusingly the "Army of Tennessee" by the Union forces) in the fierce and final offensive that eventually led to the collapse of the Confederacy. He was in many major battles such as the battle of Lookout Mountain and Missionary Ridge. He must have seen many men bleed and die.

During the drive toward Atlanta, Greathouse was promoted to the rank of Colonel, the final rank before becoming a General. His reputation as a soldier continued to grow. After many battles the Union army reached the outskirts of Atlanta. There the Confederate forces, facing grave danger, decided to launch a counter-offensive. John Hood, Confederate General from Texas was known for his aggressive leadership. Because of that aggressive quality, he was given command of the forces protecting Atlanta. In a vain attempt to save the city and ultimately the Confederacy, Hood attacked the Union army just outside Atlanta hoping to break their resolve.

On July 22, 1864, the Confederate attack was launched where Greathouse and his men were deployed. Greathouse and the Union forces repelled the attack and mounted their own counter-attack. There, at the outskirts of Atlanta, with the flag of his country in his hands, Col. Lucien Greathouse was struck and killed.

His grave quotes two prominent Generals. William Sherman, who went on to fame and infamy in his conquest of Atlanta and march to Savannah said about Greathouse, "His example was worth a thousand men." John Logan, the politician General from Illinois called Greathouse, "The bravest man in the Army of Tennessee."

He was a full Colonel. He led his troops in forty battles. He was called the bravest man in the army of Tennessee. His example was worth a thousand men. And when he died in July of

1864 he was two months past his twenty-second birthday.

Life is but a moment. Should God give you one hundred and twenty-two years, it would be but a moment in history and eternity. Passionate people understand this. They realize the hour is late and the opportunity is now. They know they must do their best in the few, brief days they have in this world. They know they must prioritize wisely if they are to make the best usage of those brief days.

Passionate people set priorities because they realize the needs of the hour. Paul spoke of priorities when he wrote, "But one thing I do: Forgetting what is behind and straining toward what is ahead, I press on toward the goal to win the prize for which God has called me heavenward in Christ Jesus." (Philippians 3:13-14) Paul recognized what passionate people of faith know: God has placed me in this world for a reason and all distractions must be set aside allowing me to accomplish that purpose.

Passion focuses on "the goal to win the prize". The needs of the hour lead passionate people to focus attention and energy towards meeting those needs. God sometimes gives us moments of opportunity that must be seized.

I recently read a book by Stephen Ambrose called D-Day.[21] The stories of this massive invasion of Normandy by the Allied Forces are amazing. So many sacrificed so much for the cause. The Allied Forces knew they would lose many men and sacrifice in many ways and yet they were willing to pay the price. Why? Because they knew the needs of the hour. Listen to the story of one of the young paratroopers who was about to parachute behind enemy lines.

Pvt. Ken Russell of the 505th had just made it onto his C-47. Two weeks earlier he had been running a high fever, a result of his vaccinations, and was sent to a hospital. On June 4 he still had a high fever, but "like everyone else, I had been looking forward to D-Day since 1940 when I was still in grammar school. Now I was so afraid I would miss it." He begged his way out of the hospital and managed to rejoin his company on June 5.

Flying over the Channel, he was struck by the thought that his high-school class back in Tennessee was graduating that night.[122]

What was your graduation night like? I can tell you I didn't give much thought to jumping out of an airplane behind enemy lines and fighting close combat with hostile forces the night of my high school graduation! But Ken Russell, and Allied leaders, recognized the needs of the hour. That recognition led them to passionately pursue their goals and objectives.

The needs of this hour are great. Our battles may be different than those faced by the heroes of Normandy, but the battles are real nonetheless. The spiritual needs of this hour cause us to prioritize our resources. The spiritual battles that loom cause us to sacrifice and serve. We have been placed in this world for this time and this opportunity and by God's grace we can fulfill God's purposes in our generation.

I sometimes feel the needs of this generation are overwhelming. I can't read the paper without seeing evidence of a world that has rebelled against God. I can't watch television or observe popular culture long without seeing the depravity and debauchery of my generation.

Steve Farrar quoted an influential preacher in London who said what I feel often about the world that surrounds me. The preacher said, "We are living in days of exceptional evil." The quote didn't surprise me. What surprised me was that the quote was by D. Martin Lloyd-Jones way back in 1959[23]. I wonder what he might say about these days.

The needs of our day are great. Spiritual apathy, immorality and blatant hostility towards the things of God seem to be on the increase in our generation. And yet there is a God who promises to be able to meet those needs and to give us hope for the future.

Passionate people set priorities because they believe in the opportunities of the day. I describe myself as a realistic optimist. I am not a pessimist who sees only doom and gloom. I am not an unqualified optimist who sees the world through rose-colored glasses. I am a realist who knows there is much evil and many problems in our world. But I am optimistic about God's ability to work out his good and perfect will in an often bad and imperfect world.

The realistic side of me keeps me passionate because I see the needs and want to do something to improve the conditions. The optimistic side of me keeps me passionate because I see what can be if God's purpose is fulfilled.

I have taught evangelism in my church for years. Nothing fuels the passion of a class for reaching people like a little success. When someone has the privilege of leading another sinner to faith in Jesus Christ they are energized. And when they tell that experience to the rest of the class the entire class is energized. Why? Because at that moment they realize that evangelism training is not an academic exercise, but an opportunity to make a difference.

A subtle pessimism can creep into any training class. "I don't know why I took this evangelism class. I've never led anyone to Christ and never will." "Why did I take this sales seminar? This stuff never works for me." When that kind of pessimism enters our thinking we lose our passion for the work. But give a salesman a little taste of success and watch out. Let someone lead their neighbor to the Lord and "Katie, bar the door!"

One aspect of passion for God's work is a realization that God gives us real opportunities. This day, this week, this year God will give you moments of opportunity. You will have opportunities to point people to Christ, to minister to needs and to encourage the downtrodden. Those moments of opportunity, wisely used, will impact real lives for today and forever. You can play a part in God's work today. And that understanding will lead you to great passion to be about the work of God's kingdom.

Passion and Work Ethic

Passionate Christians have often been known for their willingness to work. The Puritans connected hard work to their theology. They wanted to do their best for God and hard work at any endeavor became a way for them to praise him. This practice became such a part of their life and practice that we still hear of the "Puritan work ethic". Passionate people understand this work ethic.

Passionate people work hard. Perhaps no group of people understands the importance of hard work more than dedicated athletes. I am amazed by the level of sweat and blood they shed for improvement in their sport.

Tiger Woods is a pretty good golfer. Okay, he is an incredible golfer. Recently, I was listening to a radio sports program. A man who is intimately involved in professional golf was talking about the phenomenon that is Tiger Woods. He noted Tiger's great talent. But something else he said caught my ear. He said that no one he has ever seen in years of covering professional golf works as hard as Tiger does.

Why does Tiger Woods work so hard? He already has money and fame and a special place in golf history. Why not kick back and enjoy some extra time off? Why not skip a few workouts, take fewer practice rounds? Why? Because he is passionate about golf. And if you are passionate you are willing to work hard.

Passionate Christian leaders don't have to be begged to prepare. They don't need coaxing to do their best for God. They have to be encouraged to rest. This kind of Christian leader has learned to love his or her work. There are at least two reasons why. First, they love their work because they see the connection between their effort and the results they desire. They know they must work hard if they are to perform at the level they expect. All that work pays off in rewarding results.

When I work hard to prepare a sermon it is usually more effective than when I don't prepare well. And if I have to choose between preaching a mediocre message on God's love or an effective message on God's love, I think I will choose the effective one. I work hard on sermon preparation because I want the results that come with that hard work. If you study hard to prepare a Sunday School lesson the class you teach generally goes better than when you study a few minutes on the drive to church.

Most teachers enjoy teaching when well prepared. They may not enjoy all the hard work of preparation but they like the results of that hard work.

Another reason passionate people work hard is because they have discovered a joy in working for God. There is a joy that comes with effective service. Doing your best in a great task brings deep satisfaction.

Why are athletes so emotional when they win a Super Bowl or some other kind of championship? Is it because of the money or fame or trips to Disney World that come with it? Maybe. But I submit to you that their joy is more than that. It is the result of seeing all the sweat and blood and effort paying off in victory. If they could step into a championship game without any practice or effort, the victory would not be as sweet. But suffer through exhausting practices and endless drills and significant deprivation, then step onto the field and win a championship, and the emotions overwhelm.

Effective Christian leaders have learned this. They discovered the joy and deep satisfaction that comes with a job well done. And while they may not receive great honor and recognition here on earth, they are serving for the joy that comes in knowing they are pleasing God. And that motivation is greater than any paycheck or trophy or trip to Disney World could ever give.

Passionate people work smart. Hard work is important, but not enough. The goal is not how much I sweat but how much I accomplish. Passionate people are after results, not callouses. Therefore, they have learned to work smarter.

The previous section was about working hard. You might read that and decide that God wants you to be a workaholic. That is certainly not the case. Burn-out never helps the kingdom. The important thing is to learn to accomplish more by working smarter. If I wanted to move a mound of dirt I could carry the dirt by shovel to the new location. I could make trip after trip with my shovel full. I could work hard, sweat profusely and get the job done in several hours. Or, I could get a wheelbarrow and accomplish the same thing in half the time.

The leader who learns to work smarter accomplishes more. There are a couple of key ingredients leaders need to know to work smarter.

One way to work smart is to think long-term. Here at First Baptist Church of O'Fallon, we make our staff take their vacations and days off. We require them to stay away from the office some and relax a little. We know these folks are hard workers. There is no question they want to do their best and give their all. But they also need some down time. Without the time away the pressures and demands will swamp them. They will lose their long-term effectiveness without some rest.

I get many of my best ideas when I am away. When I relax I start to think better and see the big picture. Often in ministry I cannot see the forest because of all of the trees. The problems, pressures and deadlines keep me from thinking about the future. After some rest I come back refreshed and recharged.

At my marathon I saw this illustrated. Some young guys were there with military haircuts. They appeared to be in the same group. I noticed how fast they began the race, running far ahead of me quickly. I also noticed some of them again, about two-thirds through the race. They were hunched over at the side of the track in obvious pain. (I was secretly overjoyed that I passed these young "whippersnappers"!)

If they had been running a half marathon they would have done fine. But the rapid pace they set was too great for the full 26.2 miles. They did not think long-term in setting their pace.

Some of us are on this spiritual journey with family. Long-term thinking reminds us that we have responsibilities to them. Our sons and daughters need us to teach them and play with them. Our wives and husbands need us to connect with them and encourage them. Time spent with family and friends carries benefits forever and we do well to remember that.

Another way to work smart is to learn to delegate. I was a Youth Minister for a few years before becoming a pastor. It was a great time of learning and growing. My pastor during those years took me under his wing and taught me many things about ministry and life. Nearing the end of his vocational ministry, he often told me of lessons he had learned along the way in several decades of pastoral service. One of the things he taught me was about the importance of delegation.

My pastor said it was a lesson he had not learned well throughout most of his pastoral life. He was the kind of pastor who liked to do everything. He was involved in every ministry of the church. He was at every meeting. He contacted all the prospects, was involved in all the plans, made all the visits and did most of the work. As the churches grew so did his workload. But delegation was difficult. He felt guilty if he wasn't directly involved in everything in the church. And besides, others might not do the job as well.

Most church members were happy for their pastor to do all the work. And my pastor found some comfort in knowing he was such an important part of the church life. But he also made some discoveries about the danger of doing all the work himself. His effectiveness was limited without delegation. His family suffered the consequences of his absence. People in the church were not developing their own talents and ministries. And burnout was always close for a pastor who did not learn to delegate. He reminded me many times, "Don't try to do it all by yourself, Doug."

Learn to delegate; more will get done. Learn to relax once in a while; more will get done. Learn to say "no" sometimes; more will get done. Work hard, yes, but work smart as well.

Healthy Christian leaders have passion. They believe strongly in what God can and will do. They have a zeal for God and the work of his kingdom. Ask God to give you that kind of passion for your life and service. Ask the Lord for a passion for things that will matter for eternity.

Leaders who understand healthy leadership traits see their Christian service as more than a responsibility. They see it as a burning passion of their life.

CHAPTER FOUR

SACRIFICE FOR GOD'S KINGDOM

Healthy Christian leaders are willing to make sacrifices in order to benefit the work of God's kingdom.

When I was a young boy, our family moved to a very small town in Southern Illinois. My mom and dad bought a house there that needed some improvements. There was one improvement the house especially needed. It needed a bathroom. More specifically, it needed the indoor kind of bathroom.

Most modern Americans have never lived in a home with an outhouse. Trust me when I say, "You don't want to!" There isn't anything romantic or pleasant about them. When it is cold outside, the trip is exceedingly undesirable. But when it is hot, the stench is exceptionally repulsive. The first thing my Dad did upon buying the home was to begin construction on an addition to the house that featured a new indoor bathroom. What a happy day it was for the Munton family when construction was complete. After that, we never even considered buying a home without indoor facilities.

I couldn't help but think of those childhood days when on my first mission trip to Eastern Europe. In some of the places we stayed, the bathroom facilities were less than desirable. I missed my comfortable home and my sanitary bathroom. I looked forward to returning home in a few days to the conditions to which I had grown accustomed. After all, I expected something better for myself. And indoor plumbing was near the top of that list of expectations!

I met several career missionaries while I was in Eastern Europe and came to realize something amazing about them. They had willingly sacrificed many of the comforts of their past to serve God in this land. They gave up nice bathrooms and easy access to their families and many other things I expected for myself. They sacrificed and did so willingly for the sake of the gospel and the people they had been called to serve.

Not many books on leadership include chapters on sacrifice. But a willingness to sacrifice is an indispensable quality for any Christian leader. Not everyone will be called by God to leave his or her home and serve in a far-away land. But you cannot serve God without a requirement of sacrifice. One of the most challenging thoughts in all the Bible comes from Jesus when he said, "If anyone would come after me, he must deny himself, take up his cross daily and follow me." (Luke 9:23) If you follow Jesus you must sacrifice. Healthy leaders sacrifice willingly.

The sacrifices you make for the Lord cannot compare to the blessings of living for him. Sometimes the blessings come through the activities of sacrifice. But in order to follow Jesus we must be willing to deny ourselves and take up our crosses.

The Example of Sacrifice

Our family got a ping pong table some time ago. It came with instructions on how to put it together. The instructions had obviously been written by a person with very little grasp of the English language. Either that, or I was the one with little grasp of the language. Because somewhere there was a terrible failure to communicate!

I finally got it together by combining the written instructions (I think it was a poor translation of the original Mandarin) with the picture that was drawn showing the construction. The illustration became for me the model of how I was to put the table together. I needed an example to get the table put together in working order. (I did have some extra screws and such left over but I'm sure it couldn't have been *my* mistake!)

In a similar way, I need an example of sacrifice. I need to see what it looks like and what it entails. If I can get a picture of what a sacrificial life looks like I can better emulate that lifestyle. Fortunately, there is a great example in the pages of the

Bible.

The Model of Sacrifice. No one demonstrates sacrifice like Jesus. He doesn't just talk about denying self, he demonstrates it. He is the supreme model when it comes to thinking of others. He endured the cross for sinners like us. His example demonstrates to us the depths of sacrifice and concern for others. His sacrifice shows his love for us.

The cross is the great model of sacrifice. It calls me to follow the example in sacrificing my own life. Calvin Miller, speaking of the example of Christ's death said, "it is the judgment of the Cross that I should give my life as a sacrifice to the Lord, who gave his life as a sacrifice for me."[24]

By definition, most of us husbands are knuckleheads. We tend to think of ourselves first. We have trouble helping around the house. Our leisure activities come before our families. We can't seem to find the clothes basket. The list of our "knuckle-headed-ness" is a long one. I don't know about you, but I need some example of how I am supposed to live as a husband.

Probably the most helpful words to me on the subject of being a good husband are found in Ephesians 5:25. "Husbands, love your wives, just as Christ loved the church and give himself up for her." I have a model for the way I am to love my wife. My love is to be like the love Jesus shows the church. I am to give myself up for my wife as Christ gave himself up for the church. It is my responsibility to sacrifice on her behalf as Jesus was willing to sacrifice on my behalf.

How well I sacrifice on behalf of my wife is a model for my children. I am teaching them, for good and for bad, what it means to be a spouse. A good spouse is willing to "give himself up" for his or her mate. If I learn from the example of Jesus I can be a better example for my children. If I think of my wife first I can be a better husband. If I learn to sacrifice for my family and others I can be a better follower of Jesus Christ.

As a leader in ministry, you model sacrifice for others. Your partners in ministry see the example you give. Those you disciple see in your life a model, for good or bad, of what sacrifice ought to look like in their lives. The better you follow the model of Christ's sacrifice, the better off others will be as they follow your example.

The Power of Sacrifice. Sacrifice is a powerful tool in God's hand. During the early days of the church, sacrifice was frequent. Many lost their lives because of their commitment to Jesus Christ. Christians often lived in fear for their physical well-being. And yet the church grew. Tertullian said, "The blood of the martyrs was the seed of the church." Apparently, the more persecution the church faced, the greater numbers of people trusting Christ as their savior. Persecution could not stamp out the church. The sacrifice of the martyrs became a powerful call to the world to the legitimacy of the gospel. Like blowing on dandelion seeds, persecution merely spread the gospel message faster and farther. There are several reasons to suggest why sacrifice is a powerful tool for the spread of God's kingdom.

Sacrifice is intriguing. People are drawn to the unusual behavior of sacrifice. Something within man longs for the rigors and discipline of sacrifice. We are intrigued by the athlete, politician or average person who overcomes long odds through great personal sacrifice. We are amazed at the stories of those who risk.

The story is told of military recruiters who presented the benefits of service in their respective branches of the armed forces to a group of graduating high school students. Each of the four recruiters was given ten minutes to present their case for joining a particular branch of service. The Air Force, Army and Navy recruiters made passionate pitches about the advantages of their organization. Each took more than the allotted ten minutes. Finally, the Marine recruiter stepped to the platform. Knowing time was short he looked over the sea of faces from one end of the auditorium to the other. Finally he said, "I doubt there are more than three or four of you here who have what it takes to be a Marine. I want to see those few immediately after the assembly." He was swamped with applications. Sacrifice intrigues us.

I saw a special show on television recently that covered the "Ranger Challenge." The show followed the events of Army Rangers as they went through several days of rugged competition. With almost no sleep, these teams of two competed in numerous events like swimming while towing two hundred pounds of gear, followed immediately by carrying their burden across hills and valleys, or running twelve miles with massive backpacks and rifles, or maneuvering through obstacle courses in the dead of night. For several days they tortured their bodies with physical feats and challenged their minds with complex problems. It is an amazing feat of human endurance.

I am told by recruiters that shows like that actually help their efforts. Many young men and women are drawn to the incredible efforts displayed by military groups like the Rangers. These young people are often looking for a challenge and are intrigued by the sacrifice.

Have you read *Foxes' Book of Martyrs* or perhaps the newer version of the same theme entitled *Jesus Freaks?* These books tell the story of those who gave their lives for their faith in Jesus. My library contains a good number of books about people who gave up much for God's kingdom. I am intrigued and challenged by these stories. Years ago I read a book called *Bruchko*. It was the story of a missionary to South America. Everything was difficult for the poor man. He faced incredible hardships, sometimes hostile natives, great deprivation. His life was one giant sacrifice. And yet, as I read the accounts of his battles, I was more drawn to considering a missionary career than ever.

The stories of sacrifice for God draw me. They remind me to be "a living sacrifice". I am not repulsed by these difficulties, I am inspired by them. And many unbelievers in this world are drawn to them as well. In a world where many find no reason to live, some have found a cause for which they will die. Sacrifice is an intriguing topic for believers and unbelievers alike.

Opportunities for ministry often come out of our sacrifice. I've never been on a mission trip yet without the frequent question, "Why did you come?" They wonder why I would leave behind family and sacrifice my time and money. This allows me the opportunity to tell them about the love of Christ.

Sacrifice strengthens resolve. The most difficult weeks of training for my marathon were weeks one and two. Other weeks were equally as painful, but none so difficult. In training I followed to the letter the suggestions of running guru Hal Higdon. His eighteen weeks of training called for runs four days a week. Every Saturday a long run was required. The first Saturday called for a six mile run. I had successfully completed three runs of three miles each earlier in the week, so I expected to make the six-miler without too many problems. I was wrong.

That Saturday morning was the first really hot day of the summer. The heat sapped my strength and increased my discomfort. And six miles is twice as far as my three-mile runs. (Having excelled in Mathematics I know these things!) That combination made the run extraordinarily difficult, the hardest run of my training, matched only by the next Saturday.

The second Saturday run was a seven-mile jaunt. The severity of that run was exacerbated by the mountains of North Carolina. Speaking at a conference there, I was forced to run those tortuous steeps so far removed from the flatness of my native land.

Those two runs required some real pain and, yes, sacrifice on my part. I would run farther distances. I would face similar weather conditions. I would often curse the pain and toil of running. But never again, after those two sacrificial Saturdays, would I consider quitting my training. The early sacrifices had strengthened my resolve.

Have you ever felt like quitting spiritually? New believers are excited about faith. Then comes the first bout with adversity and they feel like I felt on that first hot run. When faith costs them something they feel like they are running in mountains. But if they stay faithful when they feel like quitting they emerge stronger than ever. Their resolve to follow the Lord is steeled by endurance through times of sacrifice.

Sacrifice is faith building. Due to the privilege of being able to pastor two growing churches, I have been involved in several building campaigns. And, due to being in several building campaigns, I have been in several capital fund raising campaigns. And, due to being in several capital fund raising campaigns, I have given many sacrificial gifts to building programs. I will mention more about those sacrifices later, but suffice it to say, those events have built my faith.

During each capital funds campaign, Vickie and I have prayed about what God wanted us to give. Each time we have felt God call us to give an amount that took sacrifice. But each time, God has provided for us to be able to give what we committed and to meet the needs of our church project. We are beginning to think God knows what He is doing!

Sacrifice requires some level of trust. And when we trust God we find him trustworthy. Finding him trustworthy strengthens our faith. There is a direct link between our sacrifice for God and our increased faith in God. Through sacrifice, our faith is deepened and strengthened.

Sacrifice is contagious. When I was a boy I got chicken pox. I got chicken pox because someone, perhaps my older brother, got chicken pox. As a result of my exposure to a chicken pox-infested brother, I got chicken pox. And then, being the giving kind, I gave my younger brother chicken pox. There was a whole lot of chicken pox infesting going on around our house.

That's the way a contagious virus works. Exposure to someone carrying the disease leads to outbreak. Close contact to someone with the malady leads to infection.

I think sacrifice is a contagion. Close contact to people who sacrifice for God's kingdom tends to inspire us to join in the sacrifice. We are inspired by testimonies of people giving up personal rewards for the greater reward of God's glory.

I am inspired and challenged by people's stories. Especially when I can relate to those people. When I see average, every day people like me do extraordinary things I am inspired. Being around people who are "living sacrifices" for the Lord makes me want to live the same way. It is as though the virus of sacrifice gets transmitted to us through the examples of others.

Recently, a man in our church told me about how God had strengthened his faith. He made a sacrificial commitment to the building program of our church. He and his wife prayed long and hard about the commitment they made. They felt that God wanted them to give what was for them a large amount of money. It seemed like it was just too much for them to give. But he told me how God had provided the means for him to give in some very unusual ways. He was so excited about God's provision and I was inspired by his faith and God's faithfulness.

I got chicken pox as a boy but I didn't get small pox. That's because I got inoculated. As I understand it, an inoculation is accomplished when one is given a very small dosage of the disease. The body is able to effectively fight off such a small dosage and thereby builds up immunity against the disease.

Some have been inoculated to a sacrificial lifestyle by the small doses of exposure they have received in their experience. They miss a television show that looked somewhat interesting because there was a special service at church. They pat themselves on the back for the deep sacrifice they made. They tip God's work with a small portion of their income instead of splurging on a new nose hair trimmer and call it sacrifice.

But when these inoculated Christians meet someone with a full-fledged case of raging sacrifice they are challenged. Personal contact with those who have given up families and houses and careers for the kingdom may jolt them from their life of ease. When sacrifice is exemplified by a friend, a family member, a Sunday School teacher or others they know, the contagious qualities of sacrifice can really take effect.

There is a power in sacrifice. Sacrificial living is the means by which God works through people. When we sacrifice, God is able to use us, to empower us and to mold us.

Reasons for Sacrifice

Beyond the example of sacrifice given by Christ and the

clear teaching of scripture calling us to that kind of life, there are many other reasons for us to sacrifice. Several of those reasons should be noted.

It is war time, not peace time. My parents were young when the United States entered World War II. They can remember some of the sacrifices our nation endured to help the war effort. Sugar was rationed, as were many other commodities. It was difficult to obtain tires for automobiles and tractors, even if you could get the gasoline needed to run them. The country as a whole was required to do without many helpful items. And that is not even to mention the sacrifice of mothers and fathers sending their youngsters off to fight a war. My father was drafted near the end of the war and was prepared to sacrifice more than just material possessions.

Could you imagine asking the average family in average times to give up sugar? Rioting in the streets would follow. No coffee? Giving up cappuccinos might induce widespread panic. Why the difference in reaction between the World War II generation and other generations? Some say it is merely the differences of the culture. I think it is more about the difference in necessity. When a war threatens the survival of our nation, many who might otherwise cry about sacrifice would willingly sacrifice.

We have seen that in the sacrificial outpouring of work and financial aid that poured in to help the victims of terrorism in our land. Many thought Americans were too self-centered to care about others in 2001. But threats on our land rallied us to sacrifice on behalf of others.

One of the reasons Christians need to sacrifice is because of the spiritual war we are fighting. If we think we are in peace time we are less likely to give and to serve and to work. But when we realize the mighty struggle we face we are more apt to take the painful but necessary steps to experience victory.

I remember when I applied for the armed services draft. I looked at the front page of the newspaper differently. Every time a conflict broke out I thought, "This could be the beginning of a war and I could be drafted!" I was reminded that I lived in a dangerous world and I might be called upon to sacrifice to preserve the freedoms of my nation. My perspective began to change.

I am already drafted into God's army. Every day I have responsibilities in his service. Spiritual warfare rages and God calls all who name the name of Jesus to join in the fray. If my Commander-in-Chief wants me to engage the enemy, even if that means personal sacrifice, I want my answer to be, "Yes, Lord!" There is a spiritual battle for the souls of people and I need to be willing to sacrifice to bring hope and help to others.

This world is not our home. Have you ever gone on a long trip? There is a lot of excitement about seeing new sights and enjoying new experiences. It can be relaxing and invigorating. Long trips can renew our souls and sharpen our senses. They can also drive us to the brink of insanity.

If you have ever traveled long distances in a car with young children you know some of the resultant problems. I know what it was like when our children were young. Loud whining. Frequent arguments. Incessant calls of "Are we there yet?" Crying, complaining, moaning. And that was just from me!

One of the worst things about traveling is sleeping in a strange bed. I miss my own pillows and the comfort of my own mattress which sinks at just the right spots. Strange beds have strange smells and strange squeaks. Traveling means high prices and uncomfortable settings. But I can take all that because I am not at home.

I am willing to sacrifice the comforts of home when I travel because I know the comforts of home await me when my travels are over. Similarly, I am most willing to sacrifice on earth when I am most aware that earth is not my home. One day I will be home, but this world is not my home.

When I get home, all sacrifice will end. I will be in the place God made for me. There will be no more sorrow, no more pain, no more sacrifice. But I am not home yet. And so I must be willing to sacrifice as God leads me until that time. Paul said it like this in Romans 8:18, "I consider that our present sufferings are not worth comparing with the glory that will be revealed in us." One day I will be in my home and sacrifice no more. Meanwhile, these small sacrifices are nothing in comparison to that great day.

The needs and opportunities are great. Some time ago, our church had the privilege of baptizing several men who came from Muslim backgrounds. They grew up in places where hearing the gospel is difficult. But circumstances brought them to America and into contact with several people in our church family. Our people ministered to their needs and told them about a personal relationship with God through his son, Jesus Christ. They responded to that message, trusted Jesus Christ as their Savior and Lord and were baptized in our church.

Those opportunities happen because people have been willing to sacrifice. People sacrificed to build our buildings where the truth is proclaimed. People sacrificed their time and energy to build relationships with people of another culture. And they sacrificed because the opportunity to reach these men who had never heard the gospel was so great.

In many ways, the needs and opportunities of our generation are greater than ever. More people than ever need to know of God's love. The obstacles seem great, but the opportunities are great as well. Many people are open to the gospel. Many have become disillusioned with success, affluence or fame. They are looking for answers. And we have the chance to make a difference in this generation.

Here in the United States it seems the spiritual needs are ever growing. Fewer people have clearly heard the gospel message. Fewer grow up in a faith community. Fewer own Bibles. Fewer sing the songs of faith. While that is discouraging on the one hand, it is energizing on the other. I realize the spiritual needs of my homeland are greater than ever. This leads me to sacrifice more for the sake of meeting those needs.

As I write this, it is the middle of Vacation Bible School week in my church. This year well over nine hundred workers and children are enrolled in this wonderful program. Children are singing, doing crafts and learning Bible stories. They are learning of God's plan for their lives and having a great time doing it. And for many of these children, this is the first time they have ever heard about Jesus.

More and more I meet families who have no connection to the Christian faith. They show up at our church because of a need, or an emptiness, or a longing they can't quite explain. But they have no connection to faith. They don't own a Bible and never have. They don't understand the basic message of the gospel. They have never participated in a church.

That kind of challenge motivates me. I want to sacrifice knowing my sacrifice can help us reach people with no church background. The needs are so great, the sacrifices I make pale in comparison. I can reach families who have never heard about Jesus. That kind of opportunity is worth sacrificing for.

We are making eternal investments. The fifth chapter of Mark tells the remarkable story of a man with a problem. He was belligerent. He was wild. He mutilated himself. And he refused to wear any clothes. I like the way someone described him. He is "the rude, nude dude!"

Jesus saw this man and loved him. He cast the demons out of him and set him free from the spiritual and emotional bondage that had shackled him for so long. The change in the man was incredible and immediate. He was sitting calmly, dressed and thinking clearly. It must have shocked the folks in the area to see such a transformation.

But the folks were not so happy. In fact, they asked Jesus to leave their region. They pleaded with him to leave. I have my suspicions about why they wanted Jesus to leave. I don't think they wanted to sacrifice.

When Jesus cast the demons out of the man, he cast them into a herd of swine. The pigs ran off a cliff into the sea and drowned. Those sorts of losses hurt the economy. And the people were thinking about earthly investments instead of eternal investments. They didn't want the spiritual victory if it meant financial sacrifice.

When we consider the eternal investments we make when we work and serve for God's glory we are far more willing to sacrifice. When we think only of earthly rewards, sacrifice is less desirable. When we store up all our treasures on earth, sacrifice makes little sense. But when we see the big picture and know that our sacrifice is to gain eternal investments, our work and effort is worth it all.

Too many of us think of only the moment when it comes to our lives. A joyful, sacrificial spirit eludes us when we think only of this world.

One aspect of sound investment policy it to think long-term. I have part of my vast retirement portfolio (I say "vast" to amuse my wife!) in the stock market. The stock market goes up and it goes down. Sometimes it surges forward; sometimes it drops like a lead balloon. From a short-term perspective the volatility of the stock market makes it risky. But I am not thinking short-term. I am many years away from any thoughts of retirement. (Not counting Mondays. I always think of retiring on Mondays.) So my investment strategy is long-term.

In a similar way, my spiritual investments are long-term. I know what I do for Christ today carries long-term rewards. I can make a difference in eternity. I can encourage people to surrender to Christ. I can assist people in their walks with the Lord. I can minister in Jesus' name. These things make a difference in eternity. And should the Lord require short-term sacrifices from me to make long-term investments; that is okay with me.

When we understand the eternal investment we are making we are far more willing to sacrifice. I mentioned earlier the number of capital funds campaigns in which I have participated. For ten years I was the pastor of First Baptist Church of Corinth, Texas. We had three special three-year programs during my tenure there. These were programs designed to encourage people to give above and beyond their normal tithes and offerings to meet the needs of building new facilities or additional properties.

About two years or so after I came to Corinth, we made a decision to purchase some property for future expansion of our church facilities. We decided to ask our church family, which was very small but growing, to give for three years in order to make the purchase. Everyone was encouraged to pray and to give sacrificially. I remember the surprise I had when I discovered the highest commitment made in our church was by my family. I was still going to school, Vickie was a stay-at-home mom and we were unable to make a very large commitment. We gave, believing God wanted us to sacrifice. But we certainly did not imagine that our small sacrifice from our small income would be the largest commitment!

Three years later, our church began another campaign to raise money for new facilities. Again we called on our church family to pray and give sacrificially. Our family asked the Lord to show us what we should give. God had blessed us financially and we felt his leadership to double the amount we had committed to just three years earlier. It was a great commitment and took some serious sacrifice. But to our shock, this time our family's commitment was not in the top ten of largest commitments!

What had happened in the intervening three years? How could we double our amount and go from first to not cracking the top ten? Certainly God had sent some families to our church who had greater financial means. But the primary difference was in families who had participated before at smaller levels, then greatly increased their giving in the second program.

Many families said things like this to me. "We are so excited to be able to give to this second campaign. Last time we just sacrificed a little. But we saw God bless our church and our lives. This time we want the privilege of sacrificing more for God's glory!" They saw the eternal investment they were making in the lives of people and that made the difference in their willingness to sacrifice.

Every Christian leader is going to be called to sacrifice. I came across a great quote on sacrifice and leadership in a book by one of my favorite authors, Steve Farrar. It is a quote from Johann Wolfgang von Goethe. (I'm glad I didn't have to go through Junior High with that name!) It goes like this, "He who would be a good leader must be prepared to deny himself much."[25]

If you would be the leader God wants you to be in your home, your church, your ministry or your vocation, there is no getting around sacrifice. Those committed to healthy leadership understand that.

God will call you to sacrifice as you follow him. Perhaps that will involve sacrificing some of your material possessions. Maybe it will mean you give up time or popularity. Perhaps some of you will be called to leave the comforts of your earthly home for an area of service far from the familiar. But denying ourselves and taking up our crosses daily is always worth it because we can then follow Jesus.

As a ministry leader, are you willing to sacrifice for God's kingdom? Will you set the example in your church or in your ministry? Become a "living sacrifice" for God's glory and watch the great things God will do through you.

Seven Steps to Becoming a Healthy Christian Leader

CHAPTER FIVE

PERSEVERE THROUGH DIFFICULTIES

Healthy Christian leaders stay on task
even when facing difficult situations.

I quit the team. My parents had always taught me to finish anything I started. They never pressured me to participate in any sports or activities, but if I began something they expected me to finish. And, until my senior year, I always finished. Even when the teams did poorly or the coach yelled too much or we ran until we nearly collapsed, I stuck with it to the end.

But, as a senior in High School I quit the basketball team. A combination of less playing time, disagreement with the coach and little hope of the situation improving led to mounting frustration. So, I did the easy thing and quit. Quitting was easier than practicing hard and playing in the games very little. Quitting was easier than suffering the humiliation of falling from a senior starter to a senior bench warmer. Quitting was easier than stewing on the bench knowing I could play better than those younger guys being groomed for next year. So, I quit.

Quitting may be easier, but that doesn't necessarily make it better. I have often regretted not keeping my commitment to the team and doing my best despite the circumstances. I regretted taking the easy route instead of facing my difficulties. And often I have been tempted to take the easy route in ministry.

The word "persevere" has this definition from Webster, "to persist in a state, enterprise, or undertaking in spite of counter influences, opposition, or discouragement."[26] The Holman Bible Dictionary defines perseverance as "maintaining Christian faith through the trying times of life." [26]

All Christian leaders face trying times. Every Sunday School teacher, every ministry participant, every missionary and pastor, all face difficult situations which need to be worked through. But not all leaders persist through those times.

We have all seen Christian leaders quit. Sometimes they get tired of the frustrations of dealing with volunteers. Often they are overworked and underpaid. Or worse, they feel underappreciated and taken for granted. Some quit rather than deal with conflict or humiliation.

There are different ways to quit ministry. Some drop out publicly, some privately. Some run far from ministry, some quit while staying at a ministry post. Perhaps you have known a Christian leader who is coasting towards retirement. He or she may still hold the position, but the fire and enthusiasm and willingness to take risks for the kingdom's sake are long gone. Without quitting officially, they have quit while still on the job.

The Reality of Tough Times

I once operated under the illusion that "successful people don't have problems." I guess I thought that the key to strong ministry was a paved road leading gently down hill. But the truth is that everyone faces tough times. Some have more difficulties than others (Job seemed to have more difficult times than most, didn't he?) but all face tough times.

Once in a while I see another pastor and think, "I'd like to be like that guy." They seem to have it all together. They are articulate, insightful and (most importantly) asked to speak at the big conferences. In the course of a few months I heard three very successful pastors speak. They were very talented and winsome. They had built successful ministries and grown large churches. I wanted to emulate each of them. That is, until I heard the stories of their adversity.

One of these pastors was very humorous and witty. Yet he had a strong degree of empathy and seemed to really love people. He was successful as a church leader and speaker and I wanted to be like him. Then he told the story of the death of his wife in childbirth and the pain and anguish that he went through. He discovered the depth of God's grace and God's sufficiency in life's darkest hour. The lessons he learned in those lonely days deepened his commitment and shaped his heart.

Another pastor was energetic and bold. He had great faith and had built a great church for the Lord and I wanted to be like him. Then he told the story of his early days in that church. He had serious disagreements with some influential church members on non-negotiable items. They tried to undermine his ministry and pressured him to resign. When that failed, some began to lobby to have him fired. He told about the anguish he faced not knowing whether he would have a ministry or an income. The lessons he learned in those doubt-filled days led him to greater faith in God's grace and power.

A third pastor was famous. He had built a great church and preached in large conferences. He wrote books and led conferences and I wanted to be like him. Then he told the story of opposition early in his ministry. He told of people opposing his preaching and leadership in the church. He told of being physically assaulted while in the pulpit. He noted the unfounded questioning of his motives and ethics. The lessons he learned in those painful days strengthened his patience and dependence upon God.

After hearing of difficult times faced by each of these pastors I wasn't so sure I wanted to follow in their footsteps. I had worked under an illusion that some people were exempt from life's trials.

The illusion that successful leaders don't face problems is damaging. It robs us of the recognition of the importance of perseverance. Everyone faces difficult times in this world, thus everyone needs the biblical discipline of perseverance. Healthy leaders do not live lives absent of difficulties. But they must live lives with an abundance of perseverance.

Think of the perseverance the Apostle Paul must have needed. In II Corinthians 11, Paul notes a long list of difficulties that assailed him because of his faith. He was flogged, beaten, stoned, shipwrecked and deprived. These things happened while he was serving the cause of Christ. How tempting it must have been to take the easy road and quit ministry. Yet Paul continued on, despite suffering and persecution because he was faithful to the Lord. He understood a little about perseverance.

There is a great enemy of the doctrine of perseverance and it is called "blind optimism". Blind optimists never learn the benefit of perseverance because they falsely think they will never need use of it. "Everything will work out in the end," they merrily affirm, "so no need to learn to overcome what can never occur."

A great example of how blind optimism keeps us from learning perseverance comes from the life of Admiral James Stockdale. Stockdale was the highest ranking officer in the infamous "Hanoi Hilton" where he was prisoner of war for eight years during the Vietnam War. He set an inspiring example of bravery, honor and duty during those years. He was greatly admired and loved in and beyond the military community for his service to country and his fellow soldiers.

Jim Collins, author of some excellent books on business, got a chance to eat lunch with this living legend one day. In anticipation of the event, Collins read a book authored by Admiral Stockdale and his wife. He felt somewhat depressed reading of the terrible struggles of life as a prisoner of war. At least Collins knew there was a happy ending. How, he wondered, had Stockdale survived the camp when the outcome was certainly very much unknown? Collins asked that question and Stockdale told him that he never lost faith that the story would have a happy ending. Stockdale was convinced that he would eventually get out of that prison camp and that the experience he had there would be a defining moment in his life which he would not trade for anything.

Collins had another question for Stockdale as they walked together during the interview. He records the question and Stockdale's surprising answer as follows.

"I asked, "Who didn't make it out?"
"Oh, that's easy," he said. "The optimists."
"The optimists? I don't understand," I said, now completely confused given what he'd said a hundred meters earlier.
"The optimists. Oh, they were the ones who said, 'We're going to be out by Christmas.' And

Christmas would come, and Christmas would go. Then they'd say, 'We're going to be out by Easter.' And Easter would come, and Easter would go. And then Thanksgiving, and then it would be Christmas again. And they died of a broken heart."

Another long pause, and more walking. Then he turned to me and said, "This is a very important lesson. You must never confuse faith that you will prevail in the end—which you can never afford to lose—with the discipline to confront the most brutal facts of your current reality, whatever they might be."

To this day, I carry a mental image of Stockdale admonishing the optimists: "We're not getting out by Christmas; deal with it!"[28]

Blind optimism can rob you of a harsh reality. Vision is a great thing. But to be helpful, vision must be based in reality. And reality includes difficult times. And difficult times call for perseverance.

We must never lose faith in the end, as Stockdale noted. Certainly, our perseverance is based in our faith that God will prevail and our ultimate future is secure. But faith does not keep us from facing the most difficult or "brutal" facts in our current reality. Our current reality includes tough times. And tough times call for perseverance. And everyone, even those involved in ministry for God's glory, will need perseverance.

Staying Faithful When You Feel Like Quitting

I have felt like quitting ministry many times. I even have a special name for that feeling. That feeling I call "Monday." I'm normally tired on Mondays after a long Sunday of services and ministry. Usually there is a list of problems that occurred the previous day. A ladies bathroom overflowed. A microphone went on the blink. A junior high Sunday School teacher resigned. (For some unknown reason it seems those who work with junior high students resign more often. I wonder why that is?) Someone complained that the sound system was too loud and kept him from getting a good nap during my sermon. So "Monday" and "feel like quitting" become synonyms. But "feel like quitting" and "quitting" are two very different things.

Those moments when you feel like quitting are actually tremendous opportunities for personal growth. Those are the very moments perseverance was designed to combat. Your feelings of tiredness, discouragement and frustration can be overcome by faithfulness to the task to which God has called you. And often, the potential benefits are greatest when the task is most challenging and the desire to quit is strongest.

For a number of years I ran an eight mile race with my brothers each year. It was on Thanksgiving Day in downtown Dallas and was called, appropriately enough, the Turkey Trot. We brothers trained for it each year and ran together. There was, of course, a little friendly competition between us. None of us were in any danger of setting new course records, but we did like to be faster than the other brothers. And that competition was fine. Some years I was faster than they were and some years I was slower. No big deal, really.

Then one year, one of the sisters-in-law wanted to run. She was newly married into the clan and wanted to participate since she was an avid runner. So I asked my brother how fast she was and he said she was comparable to the rest of us. Now, it's one thing to be outrun by your brothers. But, chauvinist that I am, it is another thing to be outrun by your new sister-in-law! So, with only a few more weeks left before Thanksgiving, I began to train more seriously. I could not have my new sister-in-law showing me up. What would the nephews think?

I was training about four days a week by that point. I had two rules: four miles each run and no walking. And so, with the motivation of a sister-in-law to beat, I trained. And one day I felt great. I went out hard and ran smooth. When I reached the turn-around, the second half seemed easier than the first. I finally understood why some people enjoyed jogging. Daydreams of running in the Olympics danced in my head. I'm a patriotic guy and the United States needs some good runners and I was running well. Why not?

I got back to the house after four miles and felt great. Not too tired, not too stressed. Bring on the sister-in-law!

The next run was a different story. I felt tired from the first step. My legs felt like jelly. My lungs burned immediately. I began to spit within the first quarter-mile. You know, the long, stringy spit that dangles from your lips and says "this is no fun at all and should be terminated immediately." I struggled for each step. I wanted to quit. But I had rules: four miles, no walking. I staggered to the turn-around and headed back. It seemed as though the wind was in my face both directions I ran. All thoughts of the Olympics ended and I thought only of survival. Finally, mercifully, the run ended.

A few weeks later I finished the Turkey Trot. And I am proud to say I was a little faster than my sister-in-law. Not much, but a little. And do you know which training day helped me the most? I don't think it was the day when everything was smooth and pleasant. I think it was the day that I felt like quitting but persevered that made the difference. That was the critical day.

When you face a difficulty in ministry you may well be tempted to quit. But that could be your critical day. That could be the day that you learn the lesson of perseverance and are catapulted to greater days of ministry influence. Many people quit too soon. They are tired and think they can't go on. In reality, they may be training for ministry victories that are just around the corner.

Certainly there are times to end involvement in a ministry, to find a new area of service, to direct your talents and energies in a different direction. But feelings of frustration are not always the best indicators of those times. Everyone will feel like quitting. Tiredness and struggles will cause you to have those feelings. But if God does not release you from an area of ministry, feelings shouldn't either. And those feelings of tiredness or those difficult struggles may be just a short distance from the victories that you seek.

How do you know when to leave a particular ministry? Ask yourself some questions. Do you sense God wants you to

mundane

end your current ministry? Has God redirected your passion to another ministry? Is it clear to you God is closing the door of your current ministry involvement?

Notice I didn't say anything about feelings or how hard the ministry is. If you quit every time you get tired, you will quit often in ministry. If you quit when ministry is hard, you can expect to quit soon. And by quitting you may be missing the very tool God wishes to use to train you to be more like him.

Perseverance and the Mundane

Many parts of my ministry are exciting and I enter into those tasks enthusiastically. Other parts, necessary though they may be, are less exciting. They are the mundane, the ordinary, the plain. I know they must be done, but it is sometimes hard to be enthusiastic about them.

I know the administrative parts of my job must be done. I know that. But those parts aren't as exciting as preaching, or sharing my faith, or helping someone in need, or enjoying a potluck dinner. I know sermon preparation is important if I am to preach a great sermon (hey, it could happen!), but the preparation time isn't as exciting as the preaching time.

Often, Christian leaders find themselves pouring themselves into the exciting and ignoring the mundane. It is almost a natural occurrence. Yet many of the more mundane parts of ministry are vitally important to the success of ministry.

If a preacher or teacher doesn't put time and effort into preparation, the preaching or teaching ministry will suffer. That which is tedious may also be necessary. Human nature gravitates towards the exciting and ignores the essential, but boring.

Some tasks seem mundane because they are done in private. Public events garner the accolades. Crowds pump the adrenaline. Success in the public arena is often very satisfying. After a successful public ministry, the private preparations and reflections seem so very ordinary.

Teachers and preachers enjoy, rightly so, the public opportunities of ministry. But it is the private disciplines that enable successful public ministries. The private disciplines might not jolt the adrenaline, but they determine the depth and breadth of public ministry.

May I say a word about spiritual discipline for a moment? The disciplines of developing a quiet time, or reading godly books, or prayer or fasting all require perseverance. Your feelings and enthusiasm for those disciplines may ebb and flow. Learning to discipline your mind and body to do those things when you are tired or discouraged is the critical difference in spiritual development.[29]

The alarm sounded at 3:50. Three-fifty in the morning. Three-fifty on a *Monday* morning. Do you know how early that is on a Monday? I wasn't getting up to begin my personal prayer time. (Though I guess you could say I usually have a "quiet time" at that hour of the morning.) I wasn't going deer hunting or going to the food court. No, I was going to get on an airplane to go to another state to attend a meeting.

I'm not big on meetings. Specifically, I'm not big on meetings that make me get up early on a Monday. But this was a meeting that needed to be held and I needed to be there. So, I got up, showered and dressed, ate some breakfast (for some reason Vickie didn't prepare a nice breakfast for me that morning) and went to a meeting. It was mundane, but important.

That evening I flew back home. I was tired and feeling a little sorry for myself for traveling so far and so early. And then it hit me. My father had done something very much like this many times. For a period of about two years, my father traveled one hundred miles one way, five days a week to drive to his construction job. He worked a full day and then drove back home one hundred miles. On top of that, he was pastor of a growing church and raised a family with four boys. He saw 3:50 a.m. many times on that alarm clock.

He persevered with that schedule so that he would not have to move his family. Being a construction worker, he moved his family many times and he wanted to provide as much stability as possible. Those drives were tiring and often mundane. But his perseverance meant I spent four years in the same school with the same friends and the same church.

Perseverance isn't as exciting as some other godly attributes, but it is incredibly important. God bless those who are willing to stay at the task, even the mundane tasks, for the sake of a greater good.

Thinking Long-Term

I was listening to a song recently about heaven. And heaven suddenly became so real to me. I could see the angels and hear the worship and feel the golden streets and picture myself bowing at the feet of Jesus. In that moment I was reminded that soon (even if it is decades from now it is certainly "soon" if you have a long-term perspective) I will be in the presence of the angels and our Savior. Some of what seems to matter now will matter very little in the presence of eternity. And other things that seem to matter little now will have great importance in heaven.

Perseverance recognizes the importance of long-term thinking. It knows that there are jobs to be done because those matters will affect eternity. It stays on task because of the benefits which might not be evident in the present.

There are three questions to ask yourself to determine if you are thinking long-term. These questions may help you persevere when you feel like quitting.

Question One: Is this important? Not all tasks are equally important. Is what you are doing something that needs to be done? If it is, persevering is sound long-term thinking. If it isn't, the work should be re-evaluated.

A great example of perseverance played out before my eyes over the past year. A red cardinal kept banging into the glass near my office. Under the apparent illusion that the reflection in the glass was a rival bird, the cardinal repeatedly flew into the window, wings flapping and claws scratching. There was a bang, then the irritating "scratch, scratch" of claws on window, and a whirl of red feathers flapping. This went on for months. It was a study in perseverance, but it wasn't important.

If you teach little boys and girls about Jesus, that is important. That job carries long-term benefits and will matter for all eternity. How well you teach them may carry ramifications for the rest of their lives. It may affect how they treat their children, what they choose to do for a life's work and their view of God. Teaching children will be frustrating at times. But if God gifts and equips you to teach children you can be assured that it is an important work and worth the frustrations. But banging your head against a glass for a year is not really that great of a deal.

Question Two: Is this necessary? I am not a "neat freak" by nature. I let my desk clutter accumulate. Organization and structure don't come easily to me. But taking an afternoon to organize, throw away, clean up and clear out is necessary once in a while. If I don't do those things I forget important correspondence and lose track of things that need my attention. I become less effective and more chaotic.

Finish the necessary jobs and you will accomplish more. Avoid the busy work that doesn't have to be done. But by all mean, stay on task on what needs doing.

Maybe you need to reorganize your ministry structure. Perhaps you need to get away for some planning. Perhaps you need to get personally involved in some aspect of ministry. The urgent will sometimes call you away from the needed. Long-term thinkers know they must accomplish the necessary if all else fails. They are willing to overcome obstacles because what they do is worth doing.

Question Three: Is this lasting? Will what you are doing still matter a thousand years from now? Are you investing in those things that have lasting value?

Too many live for the moment with little consideration for the future. But if we know what we do has lasting value we are more likely to persevere through any difficulties.

When our oldest child graduated from high school, my wife and I got sentimental. We began to reflect on how quickly the years go by. And it served as a time of evaluation for us. We are so grateful for the time we spent doing family things. We are grateful for the spiritual investments we have made in the lives of our children. Those things last. Pouring ourselves into family events, or ministry to others or growing in faith will last for the rest of this world and beyond. Keeping a long-term perspective is easier when you know what you are doing will matter forever.

Perseverance and Flexibility

I struggle to touch my toes. When I was young, I could bend in almost any configuration. My muscles were limber and stretching was easy. Now, my muscles are tight. Not muscular or strong, but tight. I've actually pulled muscles recently (which belies the notion that you have to have muscles to pull them!). I have lost much of my flexibility. Something very similar often happens in ministry.

Often, as we get older or gain more experience, we lose our flexibility in ministry. We become less able to adapt to changing circumstances and opportunities. We do what we have always done with diminishing results. And sometimes that leads to the "pulled muscles" of failure and quitting.

In seminary days, someone told me that there were three kinds of ministers: innovators, adopters and adapters. Innovators are the guys who see things differently. They are the ones who come up with new ideas. They come up with some brilliant plan and the rest of us say, "Why didn't I think of that?" These folks are gifted in ways most of us aren't. Their minds work in ways mine don't.

I heard one of these innovative guys preach. He was incredibly gifted and gave insights that illuminated the text in ways I had never considered. His stories were spellbinding. His application was stunning. I thought to myself, "Doug, why don't you preach like that?" But how? Step number one in following his preaching style is "Become a Genius." I can't follow his example because I can't become a genius!

Innovative people serve a great purpose. They provide programs, insights and suggestions that the rest of us don't see. But I am convinced they have a gift from God that most of us will never have. We can and should grow in our creativity. But God gifts some people with talents and abilities that others will never have. I think the innovators have been given a unique ability from God.

Innovators are like gifted artists. Anyone can improve their artistic skills by training and practice, but not everyone can become Michelangelo. Any of us can improve our creativity by practice and effort, but some are more gifted than others at innovative ideas. If we can't all be gifted innovators what is left? Adopters and adapters. Adopters are those who take the ideas of others and try to duplicate the same thing in their own context. They attempt to make carbon copies of the successes of others, usually without the same level of success. They give little consideration to context and cultural differences when adopting the programs and practices of others. Far too many ministry leaders merely adopt the ideas of the innovators without consideration for adapting to differing circumstances.

Adapters are different. They may not be on the cutting edge of innovation but they know a good idea when they see one. They differ from adopters, however, by making adjustments that fit their own ministry context. Taking the brilliant insights of others, they adapt those ideas to their own church or ministry culture.

Rick Warren, pastor of Saddleback Church in California and author of *The Purpose Driven Church* and *The Purpose Driven Life,* warns frequently of the danger of one church trying to replicate another. Every context is unique, every church culture is unique and every pastor is unique. Notes Warren,

> *You probably won't like some of the methods we use at Saddleback. That's okay. I don't expect you to since I don't even like everything we're doing! Read this book like you'd eat fish: Pick out the meat and throw away the bones. Adopt and adapt what you can use.*[30]

You can never be Rick Warren or Billy Graham or Jerry Falwell or Doug Munton. (I just put my name in there so my wife can see it with those other folks!) Your ministry can't be exactly like any other. Learn from others. Take from them what will help you to be more effective. But learn to adapt their best ideas to your setting. Your ministry will stand the test of time if you are flexible enough to follow principles rather than the latest fashion. Remember, fads will not last, but principles will.

Rigid adherence to tradition can rob you of the flexibility necessary for effectiveness. Lifeless routine can drain you of the energy and passion to persevere. Stay fresh and alert. Be open to new ideas and innovations. Never compromise on the essentials, but be open to new ways of presenting the timeless truths of the gospel. Ask God to keep you flexible in methods and programs that allow you to bear much fruit for the sake of the good news.

The word compromise sounds terrible. It virtually reeks of liberalism and apostasy. Certainly, there are many things that are not negotiable in ministry. We should never compromise on theology. We should never compromise God's truth for the sake of cultural acceptability. But there are some compromises that are acceptable, even beneficial.

Imagine you are working with a committee to draft a new policy for some aspect of mnistry. One committee member suggests each new volunteer receive five hours of training prior to service. Someone else suggests they receive six hours of training. Is this a life or death decision? Probably not. Yet some leaders will treat it as though the world hangs in the balance ready to topple should one suggestion prevail over the other.

Some leaders are too controlling. Things have to be done their way. They argue and battle over every point. The problem is, not every point needs a battle. That leader might win the battle but lose the war. Soon, no one wants to work with them because they are too inflexible and contentious.

Don't get me wrong. There are times to stand and fight. Just be sure to pick the right battles. Be flexible and willing to compromise on the issues that are not essential. Be firm and rigid on the issues that are essential. Wise is the leader who can distinguish between the two.

One of my favorite examples of knowing when to be flexible and when to be rigid comes from Lyle Schaller. He uses the model of the Lone Ranger. The Lone Ranger was a popular television show from decades ago. The masked hero fought for justice in the Old West. Those of you who can remember the show know that the hero had unusual ammunition. He was armed with silver bullets. He didn't use everyday run-of-the-mill bullets. These babies were pure silver.

Now, if you are using such expensive ammunition you must be wise. You don't waste silver bullets on dead rats or to shoot tin cans. Those bullets are saved for only the most dangerous and necessary situations.

Schaller used this story to remind us to be wise in our leadership. Every situation is not a "silver bullet" moment. Take your stand when it really matters. Be flexible on the small things. Save your silver bullets for when they are really needed.

Healthy Christian leaders learn the value of perseverance. They know they will face obstacles in life that are difficult and challenging. They know they will be tempted to take the easy road in life and to quit when times are hard. But they also know that God has called them to finish well. God calls us to stay at the task even when—especially when—times are tough.

Near the end of his life Paul wrote to Timothy, his son in the ministry. He wanted to impart some godly advice to his young friend so the subject turned to perseverance. In II Timothy 4:6-8 Paul writes these words. "For I am already being poured out like a drink offering and the time has come for my departure." Can you feel the passion in Paul's words? He knows that his life is soon to end. That's a sobering thought, isn't it? Like a drink offering that is poured out over a sacrifice, Paul's life is being emptied. Knowing the short time he has left, this hero of faith wants to impact the life of this young minister and friend.

Paul then says in verse seven, "I have fought the good fight, I have finished the race, I have kept the faith." He uses the analogy of a soldier who fights to the end. He gives the example of a runner who completes the course. Paul says in effect to young Timothy, "I have persevered in the ministry God has given me. I have left an example for you to follow"

Verse eight states, "Now there is in store for me the crown of righteousness, which the Lord, the righteous Judge, will award to me on that day- and not only to me, but also to all who have longed for his appearing." A greater day awaits. God will remember his faithful followers.

The apostle has not forgotten the reward of perseverance and neither should you. If God is in it, stay at it. Complete God's purpose in your life, come what may. Remember the great benefit to you and to God's eternal work when you live with perseverance. It is essential to godly leader health.

CHAPTER SIX

STRENGTHEN YOUR PEOPLE SKILLS

Healthy Christian leaders learn to work well
with others to benefit ministry for God's kingdom.

My father was an amazing minister. He was a bi-vocational pastor for many years. Later in life he was a Sunday School teacher. And the churches or classes he led always seemed to grow. And that growth was, in itself, an amazing thing.

Dad was never the pastor in a thriving metropolitan community. He was always in small towns and out-of-the-way places. The towns he lived and ministered in were usually stagnant or declining. And the churches he came to did not have the excellent, exciting ministries and programming that so benefit church growth. They were invariably small and often struggling. Many had been rocked with conflict and decline in previous days.

What's more, Dad did not have the qualifications necessary, by many peoples' standards, for a successful pastor. He did not have much education. He grew up attending a one-room schoolhouse. He never attended college and had only a few semesters of seminary training. He was not an accomplished orator or famed expositor. But he did have something that many ministers lack.

My dad knew how to work with people. Dad loved people. He cried with them and rejoiced with them. He calmed their fears, earned their trust and brought out their best. People were willing to overlook a lack of formal degrees and an occasional mispronunciation of the word "Mesopotamia" because they knew he cared about them and their needs. Healthy leaders value the ability to work well with others.

Developing People Skills

Some people are naturally gifted with people skills and some have to work hard to develop the necessary skills. Some of you reading this are people-oriented and some of you are more task-oriented. Some of you are shy and some of you never met a stranger. But all of us can develop our abilities to relate and work with people.

I took piano lessons for several years. I plunked away at the keys every day during my half-hour mandatory practice time. Then as soon as that requirement was over I bolted for the door to the freedom of the great outdoors. Once a week I went to piano lessons where a kindly and extremely patient woman taught me as best she could. (She is now officially qualified for sainthood.) Over the course of those years of piano lessons I got better. But I never got great.

I hear that old Mozart was something of a child prodigy when it came to music. He had a talent (not to mention a desire) that I never had. At an early age he developed extraordinary skills.

Never could I have played like Mozart. No matter how much I had practiced, I was limited in my abilities. But had I wanted to, I could have been much better than I am. Had I dedicated myself to music I could have been more proficient today. Which really isn't saying much!

My point is that you can develop your people skills if you really want to. Some may have natural talents that you don't have, but you can become more proficient if you really want to. You may be task-oriented, introverted and prone more towards a computer screen than the faces of people, but you can become better with people than you currently are.

People skills do not come easily to me. I am, by nature, something of an introvert. In many settings it is easy for me to sit back quietly and let others be in the forefront. I like being around people, but I am very comfortable being by myself. I have often been somewhat envious of those individuals who are the life of the party. That's not me (though I am fun-loving by nature). But

I have learned to develop the skills needed to work with others while being true to myself and my personality. I have plenty yet to learn about working with people, but I am growing as a people person.

Healthy Christian leaders are constantly looking for ways to better their ministry skills. Few skills will be more valuable to their ministry performance than the development of their ability to work well with people. And few things will more readily harm a ministry than a leader who never learns to work well with others.

The Importance of People Skills. Learning to work well with people is important for at least a couple of reasons. One reason is ministry effectiveness. If your ministry involves people, and surely it does in some way, you need to work well with people to be effective. All pastors say jokingly, "Ministry would be great except for the people!" But people are the ministry.

My ministry (and yours) is not about computers and charts and programs, ultimately. It is about seeing people's lives change for God's glory. People are not an interruption that keeps us from ministry, they are the object of our ministry.

Another reason for the importance of people skills is because learning to work with people causes me to develop as a person. Relating to people, even difficult people, is important to my development as a disciple of Christ. The Bible reminds us that we need other people in our lives. "As iron sharpens iron," says Proverbs 27:17, "so one man sharpens another."

My life is strengthened and sharpened as I learn to relate to others. God tends to use other people in our lives to help us become more of what he wants us to be. If I fail to relate to others because of temperament, busyness, repeated trips to the food court or for any reason, I miss much of what God desires to accomplish in my life. God wants to use the relationships I have with others to sharpen me for his service.

The Basis of People Skills. There are several attitudes

that make up the basis for developing people skills. One such attitude is value. We want to relate well with people when we value them as people. God places great value in them as his creation and we increase our desire to relate well to others when we recognize that inherent worth. People are of great worth to God and therefore should be valued greatly by those God calls to lead in ministry.

Another attitude is love. Jesus invested in the lives of people because he loved them. When my attitude matches that of Jesus, I will care about people like he does. I will show compassion and concern for others. Often, problems with people skills result from a lack of love for others. When we follow Jesus' directive in Matthew 22 to follow the greatest commandment by loving God completely, we then can follow his command to love others as we love ourselves.

A third attitude that affects our people skills is respect. I had some teachers when I was young who looked down on their students. They treated us with disdain. After all, we were just kids. But I had some teachers who treated their students with respect. They valued our opinions and ideas. They did not always agree with us, but they always showed respect to us. Those are the teachers who took the time to understand and relate to us.

Empathy is a fourth attitude which leads to people skills. This attitude tries to understand the perspective of others. People with this attitude relate to the needs and feelings of others. They understand what it is like to be lonely or hurting or frightened and they care about helping others with those feelings. When I get sick, I expect my entire household to take note and sympathize. When someone in my family gets sick, I expect them to "be tough." Needless to say, my people skills with my family suffer because of my failure to empathize with others.

Another attitude that affects our people skills is service. Leaders should see their role as servants to others, not lords who need to be served. Hans Finzel writes of the danger of a "top-down" attitude, calling it the number one leadership sin.[31] He says this attitude is "characterized by the person who believes that everyone should serve them, as opposed to them serving the others in the institution.[32] Leaders should see it as their responsibility to serve those with whom and to whom they minister. Our attitude should, Philippians 2:5-7 says, be the same as the attitude of Christ who took "the very nature of a servant".

These attitudes, like people skills in general, are attitudes we can develop. Not all are born with the same tendencies or personalities, but all can learn to love and care for people more like Jesus does. When we do, we have come a long way in developing this important attribute.

Influencing the influencers. One of the best definitions of leadership I know is "influencing others."[33] Leadership is about influencing others to do certain things. Being a leader is more than holding a position. You may be the leader in name but not the leader in practice. That is why John Maxwell and other leadership experts talk about influencing the influencers. When you influence those who influence others you are providing leadership.

When I came as the new twenty-five year old pastor of a small church in the suburbs of Dallas, Texas (First Baptist Church of Corinth, Texas) I knew there would be some leadership challenges. I also knew that I might be the pastor in name, but that is different from being the pastor in reality. The church was very small and operated in many ways like an extended family. And the greatest influence in that family was an older couple, the "pillars of the church" who had been in the church for many years. Through hard work, strong personalities and length of service in the church they were the leaders in the congregation. What they wanted was usually what was done.

I was not very smart then (I use past tense here, though some might argue for present tense!) but I was just smart enough to know that they were the influencers. If I influenced them, I influenced the church. I spent a great deal of energy trying to influence them to influence others to help our tiny church grow.

For the next several years this couple was invaluable to our congregation as the ones who led the way in many necessary changes. In those early years, we could never have moved forward as unified and successfully as we did without their influence. Their influence allowed our congregation to make the necessary changes that led to very rapid growth. I tried to influence them to influence the congregation to move forward.

Over time it became obvious that our church land, just under an acre, was becoming insufficient for our growth and future. We couldn't buy any of the land around us. Relocation was the obvious answer. But how does a church over a century old make such a bold move? This influential couple led the way in seeking and purchasing new property for a future church building. They were the "legitimizers" to the rest of the congregation that this relocation was right and best.

Over time the influence of this couple waned as our church grew. Many of the new people to our congregation did not know this couple or that they had been the "pillars of the church." I had built credibility over the years and had earned the trust of the congregation.

A critical decision faced the congregation on a very important matter related to the relocation. A brand new school had been built in our community in anticipation of growth that had not yet occurred. The school board offered to let our church meet in that building (which was much larger and nicer than the building we currently had) for the ridiculously low price of fifty dollars per week while we began construction on our new location. That was less than the utilities of our old building! It seemed to me to be so obviously an answer to our prayers. God was miraculously providing for our needs.

But meeting in an empty school was too much change for this long tenured family. They were uncomfortable with our rapid growth and suggested we stop reaching so many people. They decided to place their influence against going to the school. They assumed many would follow their lead.

Had the date been a few years earlier they would have been the primary influencers. But other leaders had risen in our congregation. A long-time couple who had served quietly for years stood vocally for the new opportunity. Some newer families who obviously loved the Lord stood with them. And I told the congregation my conviction that we had to be obedient to God in reaching people and this seemed to be an answer, a miraculous answer, to our prayers. In a congregational vote, we voted to use the school.

These long-time members of our church decided to leave our church. It was painful but we parted as friends. The church grew in the school as never before. Money was freed for ministry and to begin construction of a new building that provided more space and more growth. The church continues to grow to this day and has become a large and vital congregation with over 1,000 worshippers each week. In hindsight it became obvious to everyone that God had provided that opportunity to meet in the school.

We never would have grown had it not been for the influence of the older couple in my early years of ministry there. Their influence allowed us to grow. I was the Pastor, but I was only the leader as I led the greatest influencers in the congregation. Influence the influencers and you provide leadership to all.

Motivating People. An important part of people skills is learning how to direct others. Whether it is by directing staff, assisting volunteers or guiding people in service, ministry leaders must learn to give direction to others. A major part of directing people is motivating them for ministry. And the difficulty of motivating volunteers is that you can't use a paycheck (or lack thereof) as a motivational tool. My junior high math skills tell me that doubling the pay of someone who makes nothing is still not very high. (But remember, I was not a math major.)

So, if money is not the motivation, what is? There are different options. Some people motivate by guilt and fear. And to tell the truth, I think this works—for a short while.

For much of my early life, guilt was the primary motivation for witnessing to others about Christ. A preacher or Sunday School teacher might tell me how guilty I was if I didn't share my faith. And that is true. And I might even witness once if they produced enough guilt. But I'm convinced that guilt alone will not produce long-term witnesses for Christ. Those who share their faith consistently over a lifetime are motivated by the higher calling of love for God and compassion for people.

If you motivate volunteers through guilt and fear you will always be looking for new volunteers. Many will vote with their feet not to participate in your ministry any longer. Their enthusiasm for the ministry assignment they hold will tend to be stifled.

There is a better way to provide motivation to those with whom you work. That better way is to show them their responsibilities and opportunities. Many ministry volunteers are looking for a responsibility. They may need training. They will need encouragement. But the challenge of being responsible for something that will make an eternal difference is invigorating. Many people are looking for a challenge.

One of the best motivations you can offer people is to show them the opportunities. Jesus told his disciples that the fields were white for harvest. That is, people are ready to come to faith. He showed them the vast potential and asked them to pray for others to join in that labor of love.

Can you see the great opportunity you have in your ministry? Your Sunday School class is teaching and training people to face the challenges of life. Those attendees are part of God's plan for changing the world. Your ministry with children is preparing the leaders of the future. Your ministry in music draws people to worship the King of Kings. Can you see the opportunity? When you passionately help others see those same possibilities, many of them will join you in doing this great work for God.

Learning to Delegate

If your ministry is to grow and expand, learning the fine art of delegation can be critical to success. Yet many ministry leaders struggle with delegation. There are three types of ministry leaders regarding delegation.

Do-it-yourselfers. When something is broken at my house I am rarely called. Oh, I can change a light bulb or some other simple task. But I am not mechanically minded. My wife is far more adept at those things. She takes things apart and tinkers around and often she discovers the problem. But, if she can't fix it, we call for professional help.

Now I know there are a lot of you do-it-yourselfers out there. You rewire your house while rebuilding your carburetor. I think that is great. I would rebuild my carburetor too, if I knew what it was, and where I could find it, and how I could do it and if I cared. Those are the only obstacles I have to rebuilding my carburetor by myself. But when it comes to ministry, doing everything by yourself is not a good idea.

Some will never delegate to others because they want to do it all. They know others might not do it as well. We know what we are doing so we might as well do it ourselves. Many of us pastors think this way. We try to do everything. And we limit the potential of the church because we haven't learned to train others. The limit of your ministry is partially determined by the degree of your willingness to let others participate in that ministry.

Turn 'em loose. Another kind of delegation is turning people loose in ministry. Give that new teacher a book and let them go. Give them a manual to read and let them have at it. And then wonder what went wrong.

New workers need assistance. They need training and encouragement. They are often unsure of themselves. Many of the best Sunday School teachers in our church now started with absolutely no experience. They had a desire to serve the Lord, but no training. Our ministry heads trained them extensively. They placed them with an experienced mentor who let them observe and learn. They gradually gave them more responsibilities. Today they are excellent teachers who mentor others.

New ministry workers bring enthusiasm, but they need some training. Turning them loose without assistance will mean frustrated workers and frustrated ministry. There is a better way.

Expect and Inspect. Let potential new workers know what you expect of them up front. This saves a lot of problems down the line. If they don't want to meet those expectations, better to know that before they start.

In our church we have a class you must take before you can join our church. Our denominational background has not done that traditionally. But it has helped us in many ways. People know before they ever join what we expect them to do. They know we expect them to join a Sunday School class. They know we expect them to tithe. They know we expect them to get involved in a ministry. This allows us to start our relationship together in a healthy way. People know where we are going and can decide it they want to go on this journey with us for God's glory.

But expecting something from new workers is not enough. Elmer Towns often says, "People don't do what you expect, they do what you inspect." Delegation without accountability is not real delegation. Give away ministry to others but hold them accountable for their work. Accountability keeps minor problems minor and keeps the ministry on track.

The Benefits of Delegation. Why are most churches never able to grow beyond one hundred people in attendance? Certainly some churches are in areas of the country that don't have a population base for greater attendance. But many churches are surrounded by people yet still unable to grow beyond that barrier. May I offer a possible reason? Might it be because it is very difficult to get beyond that number of people without effective delegation?

Effective delegation allows ministry to flourish. It develops the gifts and talents of others. It allows others to make a meaningful contribution to the work of God's kingdom. And it will allow you to enjoy the ministry God has given you without sacrificing your family and sanity.

For some of you reading this book, effective delegation is all that stands between you and great ministry expansion. I'm told that two horses harnessed side by side can pull more weight than the sum of each horse pulling individually. Maybe you ought to get some new harnesses ready for the sake of the kingdom.

Dealing with Difficult People

One of the most important issues in any discussion of people skills is learning to deal with difficult people. It's easy to deal with some folks. They are kind and thoughtful. They have winsome personalities and pleasant attitudes. It is a joy to be in their presence. But have you ever noticed that not everyone is like that?

The Tendency to be Difficult. There are various categories of difficult people. Some are difficult on occasion. Some are difficult almost all the time. Some are hard headed once in a while. Some have heads so hard they can crack steel!

Difficult people may be demanding. Some are chronic complainers. Others see the bad in every situation. They might be lazy. They might even occasionally be like us.

The truth is most of us can be difficult on occasion. We have pet peeves. We have turf we feel we must protect. Past experiences can cause us to react poorly. Sometimes we just have bad days. But most of us can relate somewhat to people responding poorly because we have been there. We have been difficult to work with and complainers and immature and all the rest. I can certainly be a difficult person. (Confession is good for the soul. I feel better already!)

Realizing that we can be difficult helps us relate to those difficult people with whom we work or serve. We are far more likely to treat difficult people fairly when we recognize our own potential for difficulty.

Treat People as You Want to be Treated. I tend to treat people as they treat me instead of how I wish they treated me. A story from my childhood explains my human nature all too well.

My brother, Don, is one year younger than me. We were both little kids who played and fought together. On one occasion when we were very young, Don was playing nearby while I rested on the couch. He was goofing around with a pencil (why can't younger brothers be more like their older, more mature brothers?) when he accidentally (or so he said!) fell against me, stabbing me with the pencil. I still, to this day, have a small green mark near my eye where the pencil lead broke off under the skin.

As you can imagine, I screamed, cried and wailed. My parents rushed to console me. They told me how fortunate I was not to have lost an eye. I didn't feel very fortunate. They told me it could have been worse. "Yes," I thought, "he could have been playing with a machete." They scolded my younger brother for his carelessness. But they didn't scold him nearly enough for me. I needed revenge!

Soon thereafter my opportunity for revenge presented itself. My brother and I were setting the table for supper. He was placing the napkins, I was placing the forks. I decided to place one gently into his forehead. Four little blood spots displayed my handiwork. And Don grossly overreacted! My parents got a little excited over that one.

It has been my natural inclination to do to others what they do to me. Maybe just a little bit worse. But God tells me to treat them as I wish they treated me. And that attitude makes all the difference. It means I am to be kind to difficult people because that is what I want from them. I can be firm with them. I will still disagree with them. But I can choose to be kind to them because it is right.

Listen to Critics Without Being Broken by Them. I wonder if anyone criticized the design of the Titanic? Critics can sometimes be right, you know, even if they are abrasive or angry. It is our first responsibility to consider the merits of the criticism. But we cannot allow criticism to break our resolve.

While playing sports I received plenty of criticism. Coaches yelled at me when I made a mistake or performed poorly. In practices they screamed at me when I messed up and continued to scream at me until I got it right. And most of the time it helped me to improve. The motivation of the coaches was to get the players to perform to their maximum potential and criticism was often necessary.

I remember one football coach in high school who was especially verbose in his criticism. He was not at all shy about telling me what I did wrong and he loved to do so publicly. I was a skinny freshman with no football experience from a godly home where profanity was never used. He seemed to delight in loudly and profanely criticizing every mistake I made (and they were many!). Not only did I learn a lot about football that year, I learned new vocabulary words that could come in handy if I ever decide to become a sailor and a heathen.

Day after hot August day this coach howled his displeasure with my performance. I can still hear him screaming at the top of his lungs, "Munton, what the blank-blankity-blank do you think you're doing? You blankity-blank messed up the blank-blankity-blank play blankity-blank again!"

As painful and embarrassing as those criticisms of my football skill were, I was forced to come to a conclusion. Most of his criticisms were right. I wish he had chosen a different approach to teaching me football, but I ignored his critique to my athletic peril.

Never discount criticism outright. Even if the messenger is ugly and the method is flawed. If God could speak to a man through a donkey, he can certainly use people, good and bad, to correct us.

But what if the messenger is wrong? I've had coaches (and fellow believers) criticize me unfairly. They blamed me for the mistakes someone else made. They had a bad day at home and took it out on me. What then?

After you have considered the merits of the criticism, you make any necessary corrections and move on. Some criticisms are legitimate, some aren't. But either way, you make adjustments, if necessary, and then you move forward.

I've got to tell you how hard that is for me to do. My mother said I was the last of her four sons she would have guessed to become a pastor. Why? Was I less spiritual, less handsome, less intelligent than the others? Yes, but that wasn't the reason. She knew I was the most sensitive of all the boys.

I got my feelings hurt easier than others. I cried when I

got scolded. I pouted when reprimanded. After living with her pastor-husband all those years she knew criticism came with the territory and wondered if her sensitive son could handle it.

I have struggled with criticism for much of my ministry. Not with the part about considering the merits of the criticism. That is almost natural for me. I've struggled not to let criticism crush me. I have had to develop thicker skin.

How do you get a thicker skin? Experience helps. If you get criticized enough, and everyone in ministry will get criticized, you get more used to it and less surprised by it. I know that any time I talk about money, someone will get mad. But if I am faithful to the Bible I will have to talk about money because God does. I am no longer surprised by the criticism and can better handle it. I've been down that road before.

But perhaps the best way do develop a thicker skin in dealing with criticism is to focus on your motivation for ministry. Are your motivations right?

It was a sleepless night. I tossed and turned as I thought of the hateful letter from a church attender unfairly questioning my motives and ministry. Finally, I just poured out my heart to God. "If I have harbored improper motives unaware," I cried out to God, "reveal that to me that I might confess and repent. But if as I think, I did the best I could for the right reasons, help me not to worry about what my critics think, but about what you think."

That evening I settled an important issue. What I do as a minister is not for the pleasure of my critics but for the pleasure of my Master. No longer can I be hostage to public opinion. Oh, I still struggle with criticism and with critical people. But I know only God's opinion matters. I sleep better now.

Fight the Right Battles. Difficult people bring out the pugilist in us. When someone is tough with us, we want to box their ears, bloody their nose and knock them out. In Christian love, of course! And sometimes we should, at least metaphorically.

But pick your battles wisely. Not all critics can be convinced. Not all can be changed. Some battles are worth fighting, some aren't. Not every place is a time for "Here I stand, I can do no other." Not every hill is "a hill on which to die".

If a principle is at stake, stand. If a brother or sister can be won, fight. If a bitter heart can be softened, risk. But beware of fighting against difficult people instead of for the ministry God has for you.

Remember that the enemy is not the difficult person, but the sin that lurks behind the scene. Wrong attitudes and sinful activities are rightly attacked, but God's children, even the rebellious ones, are still deeply loved and valued by God.

A gracious response to unjust criticisms may win a brother. But if not, the kindness is still kindness. And God is pleased when we choose the good in the face of the bad. If the critic is won by our response, we are doubly blessed.

I may not be all that I need to be in regards to people skills but I know someone who is. I can observe the life of Jesus through the pages of the Bible. I can see how he was tough and kind and loving and caring. And I can learn from the Master again some personal skills that will serve me well in developing healthy leaders. If I keep it up I might just find myself enjoying ministry despite the fact that it involves people!

CHAPTER SEVEN

ENJOY THE JOURNEY

*Healthy Christian leaders learn to enjoy
the exciting journey of ministry.*

I'm a man on a mission. We recently packed the kids into the family van and headed off for vacation spots. No phones, no meetings, just relaxation. However, I forgot to tell that to my brain.

I get mission-oriented, even on vacation. We have to rush to get to the next place. "No dawdling allowed," I tell my family. "After all, we're on vacation! We've got to hurry to get there. And for heaven's sake, can't you people wait a little longer between bathroom stops? Just forty-six more miles until we can stop at a gas station that has a fast food restaurant. But we can't stop for long. Those other cars will pass us on the interstate. They'll get to our destination before we do. If I have calculated this correctly, and I think I have, we can be in and out in approximately 13.5 minutes. Okay, we're almost to the gas station. Everyone get ready... Roll, roll, roll!" And the only thing rolling is my wife's eyes.

A vacation isn't just about getting some place, it's about enjoying the time together. The vacation isn't so much a destination as it is a journey.

We often think of joy as a destination. "I'll be happy," we say to ourselves, "when I get that promotion, or reach that goal, or accomplish that feat." But I am beginning to realize that joy, like that vacation, is not so much a destination as it is a journey.

I had a doctor's appointment the day I was to start writing this chapter. It was nothing big, just a normal kind of thing. I had experienced some chest discomfort. I thought maybe it was pleurisy. But doctors are always careful about any pains around the chest, so I was given an EKG. My doctor didn't really expect to find anything as the symptoms didn't seem to match a heart problem. And I am in pretty good shape; no smoking, no drinking and still a relatively young man. (Funny, my kids don't think I am such a young man.)

It was, therefore, surprising and sobering when the doctor told me there could be a problem. He said my EKG was abnormal. Had my brain waves been abnormal I would have understood, even embraced the notion. But an abnormal EKG? No way!

My doctor told me to go directly to the emergency room at the hospital. He wanted me to get a blood test immediately. If it showed a heart problem I would be admitted, meet with a cardiologist and prepared for a possible invasive heart procedure. It might be nothing, he said, but the worst case scenario was bad. The scare-you-to-death kind of bad.

My head began to spin a little. For the first time in my life I realized it might be possible for me to die in the near future. I've had close calls with accidents before and such. But they were always over so fast I hardly considered them. And they were past tense. "I could have died back there." But this one was future tense. "I might die from this health problem." It got my attention.

The test later that day revealed that I had no immediate problem. I was grateful. But that event certainly changed my perspective and reminded me again of my many blessings. The value of my family and friends was made more evident. I am more cognizant than ever of the opportunities God gives me every day. I want to treasure them more and enjoy the wonderful journey God gives to me however long (or short) that journey may be.

If God has given you a ministry, it is a journey to *enjoy*. Not just for you to enjoy someday, though heaven's reward is exciting, but a journey to enjoy each day. If you will find joy in the journey, your ministry will be more effective and fulfilling. It will be more effective because you will stay involved longer while being less stressed. It will be more fulfilling because you will notice each victory and each miracle along the way. And you will be well on your way to discovering a healthy leadership style.

Creating a Climate of Contentment

There's an old story that says Rockefeller, the richest man in the world at the time, was asked how much more money he needed to be content. "Just a little more," came the reply. Isn't that how many people feel? We can't get quite enough.

Joy remains elusive when discontent settles in our psyche. The journey never has enough to satisfy; happiness remains just beyond our grasp. Finding contentment is a key to enjoying the journey of ministry God has for you.

The Bible reminds us of the importance of contentment. I Timothy 6:6 says, "godliness with contentment is great gain." If I live a godly life and find contentment, I am spiritually wealthy. Verse 8 of that same chapter says, "But if we have food and clothing, we will be content with that." Contentment is God's desire for his children.

The Beguiling Nature of Coveting. If modern society was choosing the Ten Commandments, I don't think they would choose a prohibition of coveting as one of them. Coveting just doesn't seem that big to make the "Top Ten" for our sensibilities. But God, knowing the condition of the human heart, chose this sin as a critical danger for his followers.

Perhaps one of the reasons for God's warning against coveting in the Ten Commandments is because of our tendency towards it. And so we are warned of the damage done by coveting our neighbor's house or wife or possessions.

The New Testament warns us as well. I Timothy 6:9-10 says,
People who want to get rich fall into temptation and a trap and into many foolish and harmful desires that plunge men into ruin and destruction. For the love of money is a root of all kinds of evil. Some people, eager for money, have wandered from the faith and pierced themselves with many griefs.

The danger of coveting is real. Even believers are in danger of placing too much value on things that last only for the moment. We can wander from the faith. A successful career woman is too busy for church and ministry because she can get just a little more. When her life becomes shallow and empty she may recognize she has wandered from the faith. We can pierce ourselves with many griefs by coveting. I think of the businessman who ignores his family to get just a little more. When the children rebel from this neglectful parent he is pierced with grief.

Coveting may be one of the "besetting sins" of our culture. In former days, Christian leaders used that term to speak of sins that were rampant and became almost second nature. These particular vices were, therefore, extremely difficult to delete from one's life. Coveting is much like that in our day.

We hardly notice coveting. It is almost acceptable within the church. Our commercials encourage us to covet. But coveting damages us in many ways. Let me note six companions of covetousness. These six sins go hand in glove with the sin of coveting.

The first companion of coveting is a focus on jealousy. "Why should my neighbor have the new riding lawnmower?" When I was young, jealousy was such a part of my life, I think I would rather we all got no dessert than to get one piece of cake while my brothers got two. The very thought of my brothers getting more than I did seemed more repugnant than the idea of my going without.

A second companion of coveting is greed. God's blessings are not given to us to horde, like a modern Ebenezer Scrooge. Greedy people are never satisfied. Their thirst for more is never slated. Greedy people are always hungry but never full.

A third companion is a lack of generosity. God commands us to be generous. But if I am generous to others I might not be able to buy that riding lawnmower to keep up with my neighbor. Coveting is focused on self while generosity focuses on others. Coveting says, "What can I get?" while generosity says, "What can I give?"

Becoming a generous person is one of the surest guards against coveting. Generous people see material possessions as a means to bless others rather than goal to achieve. Generosity forces us to think of others and takes our attention from ourselves.

A fourth companion of coveting is an absence of gratitude. I will say more about gratefulness later. But coveting focuses on what we don't have, instead of being thankful for what we do have. Our thoughts are on what we have not yet grasped, keeping us from considering how we have already been blessed.

A fifth companion of coveting is a drift from godliness. I Timothy 6:10 says that coveting can cause us to "wander from the faith." We might scarcely recognize the drift at first, but any current leads us away from something. Our eagerness for possessions puts us on a current away from God. Possessions can become idols, which pull us from our rightful worship of Christ.

A sixth companion of coveting is a lack of contentment. How can we be content if we are focusing on those things we don't possess? And without contentment, how can we experience real joy in the journey?

My parents always warned me to be careful whom I hung around. My companions would influence me, whether I recognized it or not. Beware the companions that hang around covetousness, lest you find yourselves influenced by them.

Count Your Blessings. It's funny what causes you to recognize your blessings. When things are going well, you hardly notice the many wonderful gifts from God. And then when things are at their toughest, you are keenly aware of the good. Such was the case in one of the pivotal moments of my father's life.

Dad was working in construction when he got the draft notice. It is rare that a man gets drafted into the army twice, but such was the case for my father. He was drafted at the very end of World War II. The war was winding down by the time Dad was drafted the first time. He went through basic training and some short assignments in the States before being discharged. But because he had not been in for a full two years, he was eligible to be drafted when the Korean conflict began to heat up.

My father left the familiar surroundings of the Midwest and found himself in a war in Korea. Well, technically it was a conflict, not a war, but that distinction doesn't matter much when bullets are being shot at you! It was a difficult time physically and emotionally. Many men struggle with their faith in times like that.

One day Dad had some time away from the worries and concerns of warfare, and had some time by himself to rest and reflect. So he went to the top of a lonely hillside and did something that changed his life. He started counting his blessings.

What an odd place a war zone is for someone to count his blessings! One is more likely to count his complaints than his blessings under such conditions. But not my Dad! He counted his blessings. And his perspective and his faith were forever altered. It was during that time that God reconfirmed his call to my father to preach the gospel. Dad's faith was deepened and strengthened. It was definitely an important milestone in his journey of faith.

Maybe you should take some time to count your blessings. This may not seem like the time. You are busy, you are tired, you may be surrounded by the enemy. But perhaps this is the very best time for you to find a hillside or a closet where you can begin to list the many things God has done for you. Perhaps your war zone will turn into an altar as you count your many blessings.

Those blessing lists can become quite long once they are started. Our blessings are often more numerous than we imagined. Gratefulness usually follows such a list. And contentment typically follows an attitude of gratefulness. And joy in our journey of ministry is never found without contentment.

Adapting to circumstances. Some say, "I would be content if my circumstances were different." Paul said in Philippians

4:11, "I have learned to be content whatever the circumstances." The key to contentment is never the nature of our circumstances. Paul said he was content whether he had plenty or little, whether he was hungry or well fed. The key to his contentment was, "I can do everything through him who gives me strength." (Phil. 4:13)

Sometimes the more we have, the more we think we need to be content. Greater material blessings can lead us to greater material desires. After speaking about tithing one Sunday, a man spoke to me about the subject. He said, "It is hard for me to tithe because I make a lot of money." I suggested to him, "Let's pray that God will let you make less money so it will be easier for you to tithe." He didn't like that idea very much!

Don't be fooled into thinking that satisfaction is just around the corner as soon as another accomplishment is reached. Ministry leaders may think they will be content as soon as their ministry reaches a certain level. Your contentment as a ministry leader is not dependent upon reaching more people or having more funds or attaining more goals. Your contentment is a choice.

Circumstances like imprisonment (the apostle Paul) or warfare (my Father) have little to do with genuine contentment. People who are content remember that God is with them in prisons and on battlefields. They know that God can use them in any situation. And they consciously choose to focus on the presence of Christ rather than the problems of life.

Contentment does not equal complacency. Did you read the chapter on passion? I am all for passionate ministry leaders who lead passionate ministries. God wants your best and less than your best should not masquerade behind the idea of contentment. Real contentment recognizes that we do what God calls us to do with vigor and purpose. But we recognize that all blessings come from God. And we are, therefore, content whatever the circumstances when we have done our best for his glory.

Taking the Journey with Others

I love Fridays. It's my day off. I sleep late, then take my kids to school. I read my Bible and the paper. Then it's off to Sam's Club (they give out free food samples!), maybe a little shopping, a quick lunch at *Chick-Fill-A* or somewhere and driving around looking at houses. And you know what makes all that worthwhile? I get to do it all with my wife. Fridays wouldn't be nearly as enjoyable if it weren't for her companionship.

One of God's greatest gifts to us is the opportunity we have to enjoy our journey of faith and ministry with other people. Perhaps one of the saddest sentences from the Apostle Paul is found in II Timothy 4:11. Paul is in prison. Demas has deserted him. Crescens and Titus are busy in other cities. Other friends are serving in ministry in various places. And Paul says, "Only Luke is with me." He misses his other friends and co-workers in ministry. He urges Timothy in verse nine, "Do your best to come to me quickly."

The journey of faith and ministry is best enjoyed in the company of others. There are certainly times to be alone with God. But God made us with the need for fellowship. Relationship with others can bring joy and fun to your life. Every relationship you form can be a blessing to your life, but there are three groups of people I especially want to note and encourage you to enjoy.

Take the Journey with your Family. A wise man told me early in my ministry about the danger of prioritizing ministry over family. He suggested that God should be first, my family should be second and my ministry should be third. That makes biblical sense and sounds simple. But it is very easy, especially for those of us in a vocational ministry, to get so busy with ministry that we ignore our families.

My day off is so valuable to my relationship with Vickie. We get to spend some relaxing time together and just hang out. It certainly lessens the chance of any resentment building up because ministry responsibilities keep us apart. In deer season she doesn't mind that I do some early Friday morning hunting because I try to do a lot of what she enjoys on the other Fridays. And conveniently, we enjoy many of the same activities. If you are in a full-time vocational ministry, you need a day like that. In fact, you need a day like that under any circumstances.

For those of you who are married, do you still date your spouse? I think you ought to do that about once a week. I talk to many couples that haven't had a date since Junior was born fourteen years ago! Go to dinner, play miniature golf or test the new line of chain saws together. (You know how chicks dig power tools!) It doesn't matter what it is. Just do something with your spouse that he or she will enjoy and take the journey of faith and joy together.

May I give some words of advice to you ministry leaders who have children? First, never ask your children to behave because you are a ministry leader or because it will embarrass you if they misbehave. They should do right because it is right. It has nothing to do with embarrassing or praising you. They should follow God because it is right and good and because God calls for our obedience. Children of ministry leaders have enough pressure without the additional pressure of enhancing or harming your ministry leadership.

Second, love your children unconditionally. Let them know you love them whether they do well or not. They need to know your love is not contingent upon their success or failure or even upon their right or wrong choices. Certainly you must discipline them if you love them and correct them when they are wrong. But be their greatest cheerleader and leading advocate.

You won't have a perfect family any more than you will be a perfect family member. But if you will take your family with you, you will enjoy the journey of faith far more. Besides, *someone* has to provide for your nursing home care!

Take the Journey with Friends. God has blessed me with some tremendous friends over the years. They make my journey of faith more fun. I have friends from long ago (they know my frailties, weaknesses and weirdness and are *still* my friends) and some friends who are new. Do you realize some of your best friends in life may be people you haven't yet met? How exciting!

My life has been so blessed by sharing it with friends. A local newspaper did an interview with me some time ago. They asked me whom I would most like to meet. Off the top of my head I named some folks I thought I would like to meet: legendary (and now deceased) sports announcer Jack Buck and national newspaper columnist George Will were among them. One of my friends in the church read that article. He worked hard, pulled some strings and arranged a meal with Jack Buck and got George Will to write a personal note to me in one of his books. I was blown away by the effort of this friend on my behalf.

One of my closest friends is a man I met in seminary days named John Avant. He and I studied together, prayed together and dreamed together. And we have had our share of laughs and comical adventures.

Some years ago, John and I went on a fishing trip together at a ranch outside of Brownwood, Texas. It was a big ranch, even by Texas standards. We had not seen another home for miles before we got to the ranch house. The owners weren't home but had given John directions to a large "tank" where we could fish. (In Texas, "tanks" are what other regions call "ponds". It is quite confusing when you first hear someone talk about fishing in a tank. "How sporting can that be?" we wonder.)

After getting lost on this massive ranch we finally found the tank about two miles from the ranch house. John backed the pickup truck he borrowed down to the fishing spot and we enjoyed a great time of fishing. But as it got toward sunset, we decided we should head back. After getting lost on the way in, we wanted to be sure to find our way out.

We got in the truck and tried to start it. It wouldn't start. It was out of gas! John had not bothered to check the gas gauge on the borrowed pickup and didn't realize how low it was. There was nothing to do but walk back to the ranch house, praying the owners were home.

The moment we got out of the truck and began to walk, John started talking about snakes. "This is rattlesnake country," he noted, "and dusk is the time they come out to feed. And here we are in tennis shoes." I laughed at John's cowardice. You almost never see snakes in the wild. As we walked along, I joked about snakes and John's fears and the absurdity of running out of gas in the middle of nowhere. And then I saved John's life.

Well, I don't know if I saved his life, but I saved him from getting bitten by a rattlesnake. Because as we walked along, I suddenly saw a large rattlesnake stretched out across the dirt road. John was about to step on its tail when I yelled "Snake!" and pushed him just enough to cause his foot to miss the snake's tail by an inch.

When John saw the rattler at his feet he screamed like a little girl! He jumped and shrieked and danced around, scared half to death. Now I found that extremely funny for some reason, and questioned John's manhood. But we both found it odd that the snake had not moved. Perhaps it was dead.

So I got a little pebble and tossed it at the snake. I missed by a fraction of an inch, yet the snake didn't move. Maybe it *was* dead. I got closer and tossed another pebble. This one landed on the snake and the snake came alive! It hissed (I didn't know rattlesnakes hiss until that moment) and struck at me. This time *I* screamed like a little girl!

We eventually made it back to the ranch house and to safety. I won't even tell you about the cow patty we thought was a coiled snake, or the black bull we stumbled to within inches of in the dark, or the rancher and his gun demanding to know who was sneaking up to his ranch. It was all quite terrifying. But we sure did build some memories!

Take some friends with you on your journey. They will make the hard days a little easier and the other days more enjoyable. Ask God to bless you with some great friends you don't even know yet, and treasure the friends you already have. And perhaps most importantly, be a friend to someone.

Take the Journey with Fellow Ministers. No one understands a Sunday School teacher or missionary or men's ministry leader like another Sunday School teacher or missionary or men's ministry leader. Other leaders in ministries like yours understand some of your challenges and struggles. They have been there and done that and they make excellent companions on this journey of faith.

One of the greatest joys of being the Pastor of my church is that I get to work with some of the finest people in the world. They are friends as well as co-laborers. We have gone through the good and the bad together and their partnership makes our journey of ministry so much more pleasant. And we have so much fun together it hardly seems fair to get paid. (But don't tell our personnel committee that!)

A word must be said about mentoring. If you have been in ministry for a while, one of the greatest things you can do for the kingdom is to be a friend and mentor to someone who is new in ministry. Churches are notorious for commissioning a new ministry leader with a back slap, a manual and a "Go get 'em!" Then we let him or her learn the lessons of ministry leadership with no assistance or personal guidance.

Ministry leadership can be a lonely place. I am so grateful for those few occasions when some older, wiser pastor spent some time with me. I am determined to do that for others. (Getting older is easy; it's the getting wiser that worries me!)

Befriend a new Sunday School teacher. Spend some extra time with a new ministry leader in your church or para-church organization. By doing, so you will enhance the work of God's kingdom and perhaps gain a partner who will bring your ministry journey more joy and satisfaction than ever. And you might even learn something from them.

Stay Fresh on the Journey

Years ago I was to be the guest speaker at a church in another state. No one in that church knew me, so I saw it as a perfect opportunity to experience a Sunday School class from a visitor's perspective. I arrived at the church just before Sunday

School was to start, and began to search for a class. No one was there to help a poor guest. When I finally did find someone they seemed surprised that I wanted to attend a class. But they dutifully showed me to my room.

I was taken to a classroom with peeling paint. There were a few other adults there who looked as though they were bored senseless. I introduced myself as a visitor. They didn't seem to care. I sat down and the teacher began the class.

She was a nice lady, I'm sure. But this Sunday School teacher could not have been less excited about teaching God's Word. She started the class by informing us (in the kind of monotone voice usually reserved for career government workers waiting for their pensions) how our lesson was much like the lesson from last week. And, she noted, the lessons had been very similar for several weeks. "I don't know why they have these lessons for us that are so much alike, week after week. But I guess we should go through it all the same." Boy, that sure gets a guest excited about the day!

The next hour was the longest I've ever known. I saw my life pass before my eyes. Twice. The whole thing. I kept saying to myself, "Don't fall asleep, Don't fall asleep." Most of my classmates had long since succumbed to the subtle call of slumber. When the class ended (mercifully), the teacher said, "I'll see you next week." I thought to myself, "You won't see me back in this class unless God tells me to by writing it in the sky. And then only if he writes it in buttermilk!"

That Sunday School teacher may have been filled with enthusiasm at one time. But that time was long gone. Perhaps she was burned out or tired of ministry. She certainly had no freshness or enthusiasm in her teaching any longer.

Staying fresh in your ministry is vital if you are to have joy in the journey. Don't let yourself get bored or jaded in ministry leadership. Ministry is too important! There are some steps you may take to keep that ministry freshness.

I want to learn something today. Freshness in ministry over the long run requires a ministry leader who is a lifetime learner. And every day is an opportunity to learn. Those who stop learning begin the slow march toward boredom and dullness. But learners can find something new and fresh and exciting each day.

There are several things that can keep you fresh. One of the easiest is to be a reader. I dare to say that all seven of you who read this book will get something out of it! Books can open your mind to new ideas and new ways of thinking. If you are a speaker, books can provide fresh ideas for stories and illustrations.

I look for sermon illustrations in every book I read. If I come across a story that I might use, I underline it and make a series of marks that tell me how good I think that anecdote or quote is. That practice has helped me keep fresh ideas and illustrations in my preaching ministry.

If you aren't a big reader, you can get audio books these days. And on those long commutes you may be less likely to explode with road rage when that sports car cuts you off if you are listening to a good book or tape. (Have you noticed that when they drive too fast they are maniacs, and when they drive too slow they are idiots?)

Another way to stay fresh is to attend a conference or visit another church or ministry site. I almost always get some good idea or new insight when I visit another church. I learn from others at conferences. Most of my good ideas are things I've taken from other people. (The bad ideas are usually my own.)

Today is a great day to learn something new. Read a book, pop in a tape, check out a new ministry website. Try something new, take a risk, sharpen your mind. Today is a great day to roll down the windows and let in some fresh air on this journey of faith.

Get some Rest and Relaxation. I write this section after just taking a nearly four- week sabbatical my church graciously provided. In my first seventeen years as a Pastor, I don't think I ever went two Sundays in a row without preaching. I was off four Sunday mornings in a row during this sabbatical.

I've got to admit that I felt kind of guilty. But I got over it. (I decided I felt less guilty when I was at the beach.) Now I feel more rested and relaxed than I have felt in years. I didn't realize how stressed and tired I was until I got away and got unwound.

I spent time alone with God. I enjoyed down-time with my family. I slept a lot. And I feel more excited about ministry and more focused on God's purpose than I have in years. My purpose is clearer and my enthusiasm greater, all because I got some much-needed rest. It seems as though I see the big picture a little more clearly now. It gets hard to see that forest when all the trees get in the way. And I am ready to plunge back into ministry with both feet.

Maybe a reason we lose *enthusiasm* in service is because we are *exhausted* in service. A short break can restore that vision and joy. If you try it you may feel guilty for a while. But trust me, you will get over it!

Stress is a funny thing. It sneaks up on us without our knowing it. Soon we have difficulty functioning clearly. We start complaining and snapping at folks. And we don't even know why. Ministry has become a drudgery instead of a delight.

Dr. Munton prescribes a little rest and relaxation for that malady: *Take two naps and call me in the morning.*

Finishing Strong

Here are my future plans. I plan to live to be one hundred years old. I plan to be a Pastor into my nineties and still preaching when I turn one hundred. That may not be God's plan. Perhaps he won't allow me to live in this world that long. That's fine, because heaven is sweet. And many of those plans are out of my control. Maybe I will lose my grasp of reality before I get that old. I sometimes feel it slipping away already! Maybe my health will break. Who knows? But I know I want to finish strong.

I read Steve Farrar's book *Finishing Strong* for the second time, and it scared me all over again. He told of the many ministry leaders who started well and then abandoned their faith, abandoned their morals or abandoned ministry altogether. It is a common story.

Farrar told the story of three men who started in ministry at the same time. One was Billy Graham, one was Chuck Templeton and one was Bron Clifford. Some thought Billy Graham the least talented of the three. Yet he is the only name most of you will recognize. What happened to the other two young ministers who in 1945 were possibly more famous or gifted? They did not finish strong. By 1950, Templeton no longer believed the gospel message and left orthodox faith and ministry. By 1954, Clifford had left the ministry, abandoned his wife and children, turned to alcohol and died of cirrhosis of the liver.[34] They started well but finished poorly.

That should make all ministry leaders a little nervous. We are all capable of leaving ministry and committed faith. The fall could be dramatic or subtle, but the result is the same. Finish well this race God has given you.

There seems to be a correlation between joy and strong finishes. If you enjoy your ministry leadership you are more likely to finish well. If you are finishing your ministry well, you will find greater joy in your journey. They go together.

I love older ministry leaders who are finishing well. One of our family favorites was on old pastor and evangelist named Eddie Lomelino. Brother Lomelino, as we called him, was physically unable to get around very well. But he loved his large garden and his beautiful flowerbeds. So our family helped him with those things. And he paid us richly in stories from his past punctuated by his high-pitched and frequent laughter. You couldn't be around him without feeling better. His love for God was evident and I learned much from him without even realizing it. He finished well.

Recently, a woman in our church who is well into her eighties came up to me all enthusiastic. She said, "Pastor, I am so excited! I just found a new ministry to be involved in!" She loves children and loves the Lord. She connected with our New Believer's Class for children who recently professed faith in Christ. She is now a personal mentor for children for several weeks each time the class is taught. She is finishing well.

The Bible says in Philippians 4:4, "Rejoice in the Lord always." And as though it isn't enough to say it once, Paul states again, "I will say it again: Rejoice!" And remember that Paul wrote those words while in prison. Joy is a choice you make. Your decision to find joy in the ministry God has given you is not based on your circumstances.

Ministry leadership is sometimes hard but always rewarding. Take some time to enjoy the wonderful gift God has given you in allowing you to be involved in his work through ministry. Find the wonderful joy God has for you in this journey of faith. Healthy leaders learn to enjoy the wonderful journey of life and ministry.

FOOTNOTES

CHAPTER 1

[1]Bill Hybels used this definition for a book on integrity. See Bill Hybels, Who You Are When No One's Looking: Choosing Consistency, Resisting Compromise, (Downer's Grove, IL: InterVarsity Press, 1987).

[2]Jeremiah 33:3. Numerous other scriptures encourage frequent and open prayer.

[3]The story is told more fully, and in greater context, in a book. See John Avant, Malcolm McDow and Alvin Reid, eds., Revival: The Story of the Current Awakening in Brownwood, Ft. Worth, Wheaton and Beyond, (Nashville: Broadman and Holman Publishers, 1996), 83-94.

[4]See Matthew 6:5-13.

[5]J. Edwin Orr, The Fervent Prayer: The Worldwide Impact of the Great Awakening of 1858, (Chicago: Moody Press, 1974), vii.

[6]Roy Fish to Douglas W. Munton, July 31, 1994, transcript in the hand of Doug Munton.

[7]For a more detailed account of these revival times, see my chapter "Igniting the Flame: Spiritual Awakening in America", in Tim Beougher and Alvin Reid, eds., Evangelism for a Changing World, (Wheaton, IL: Harold Shaw Publishers, 1995), 183-196. For a much more comprehensive work on these times of revival see the excellent book by Malcolm McDow and Alvin Reid, Firefall: How God Shaped History through Revivals (Nashville: Broadman & Holman, 1997).

[8]For more information on this revival see Edwin Scott Gaustad, The Great Awakening in New England (New York: Harper and Bros., 1957); and Alan E. Heimert and Perry Miller, eds., The Great Awakening: Documents Illustrating the Crisis and Its Consequences (New york: Bobbs-Merrill, 1967) and McDow and Reid, Firefall, 203-226.

[9]Albert H. Newman, A History of the Baptist Churches in the United States (Philadelphia: American Baptist Publication Society, 1898), 271.

[10]As with all these revivals, it is difficult to give precise dates for beginning and ending times because of different criteria that may be used. Some, like J. Edwin Orr, divide this revival time into two different revival times. McDow and Reid use the dates 1787-1843 in Firefall, 227-249.

[11]To see more on the Second Great Awakening see Orr, The Eager Feet: Evangelical Awakenings, 1790-1830 (Chicago: Moody Press, 1975); Keith J. Hardman, Charles Grandison Finney, 1792-1875: Revivalist and Reformer (Syracuse: Syracuse University Press, 1987); and McDow and Reid, Firefall, 227-250.

[12]Orr, The Awakening of 1857-58 in North America (Privately printed, 1983), 10. See also Orr, The Fervent Prayer: The Worldwide Impact of the Great Awakening of 1858 (Chicago: Moody Press, 1974); Roy J. Fish, When Heaven Touched Earth: The Awakening of 1858 and Its Effects on Baptists (Azle, TX: Need of the Times Publishers,1996); and McDow and Reid, Firefall, 251-274.

[13]Orr, The Flaming Tongue: Evangelical Awakenings 1900-, 2d ed. (Chicago: Moody Press, 1975), 191. For more on this revival period see McDow and Reid, Firefall, 275-298.

CHAPTER 2

[14]Jim Cymbala, Fresh Faith: What Happens When Real Faith Ignites God's People (Grand Rapids: Zondervan Publishing House, 1999), 16.

[15]Peter Wagner, Strategies for Church Growth, (Ventura, CA: Regal Books, 1987), 32-33.

[16]Rick Warren, The Purpose Driven Church (Grand Rapids: Zondervan Publishing House, 1995), 64.

[17]John Maxwell, Developing the Leader within You, (Nashville: Thomas Nelson Publishers, 1993), 29.

[18]Joseph M. Stowell, Eternity, (Chicago: Moody Press, 1995), 9.

CHAPTER 3

[19]See Luke 5:27-31. Also Matthew 9:9-13 and Mark 2:13-17.

[20]D. T. Niles, That They May Have Life (New York: Harper & Brothers Publishers, 1951), 96.

[21]Stephen E. Ambrose, D-Day June 6, 1944: The Climactic Battle of World War II (New York: Simon & Schuster, 1994).

[22]Ibid., 198.

[23]Steve Farrar, Get in the Ark (Nashville: Thomas Nelson Publishers, 2000), 25.

CHAPTER 4

[24]Calvin Miller, Once Upon a Tree: Answering the Ten Crucial Questions of Life (West Monroe, LA: Howard Publishing Co., 2002), 146-147.

[25]Quoted in Steve Farrar, Getting There: How a Man Finds His Way on the Trail of Life (Colorado Springs: Multnomah Publishers, Inc., 2001), 121.

CHAPTER 5

[26]Webster's New Collegiate Dictionary (Springfield, MA: G. & C Merriam Company, 1975), 855.

[27]Gerald L. Borchert, Trent C. Butler, gen. ed., The Holman Bible Dictionary (Nashville: Holman Bible Publishers, 1991), 1096.

[28] Jim Collins, Good to Great (New York: Harper Business, 2001),85.

[29]See Don Whitney's excellent book, Spiritual Disciplines for the Christian Life (Colorado Springs: Navpress, 1991).

[30]Rick Warren, The Purpose Driven Church (Grand Rapids: Zondervan Publishing House, 1995), 71.

CHAPTER 6

[31]Hans Finzel, The Top Ten Mistakes Leaders Make (Wheaton, IL: Victor Books, 1994), 22.

[32]Ibid., 29.

[33]John Maxwell uses this definition as does Finzel, The Top Ten Mistakes Leaders Make , 16 and others.

CHAPTER 7

[34]Steve Farrar, Finishing Strong: How a Man Can Go the Distance (Sisters OR: Multnomah Press, 1995), 4-5.

Seven Steps to Becoming a Healthy Christian Leader